Scrapbooking
for the first time™

Scrapbooking
for the first time™

Rebecca Carter

Sterling Publishing Co., Inc.
New York
A Sterling/Chapelle Book

Chapelle Ltd.

Owner: Jo Packham

Editor: Leslie Ridenour

Staff: Marie Barber, Ann Bear, Areta Bingham, Kass Burchett, Rebecca Christensen, Brenda Doncouse, Dana Durney, Marilyn Goff, Holly Hollingsworth, Susan Jorgensen, Barbara Milburn, Linda Orton, Karmen Quinney, Cindy Stoeckl, Gina Swapp

Special Thanks

Several projects in this book were created with outstanding and innovative products provided by the following manufacturers and retailers: **Lasting Impressions** of Bountiful, Utah, for embossing products; **Pebbles In My Pocket** of Orem, Utah, for unique papers, photo corners, and valuable information on color tinting; **Keeping Memories Alive** of Spanish Fork, Utah; and **Provo Craft** of Provo, Utah for a wide variety of scrapbooking products—especially Rebecca's own designs.

10 9 8 7 6 5

A Sterling/Chapelle Book

Published by Sterling Publishing Company, Inc.
387 Park Avenue South, New York, NY 10016
© 1999 by Chapelle Ltd.

Printed in China
All Rights Reserved

ISBN 1-893749-37-1

If you have any questions or comments, please contact:

Chapelle Ltd., Inc.
P.O. Box 9252
Ogden, UT 84409
Phone: (801) 621-2777
FAX: (801) 621-2788
e-mail: Chapelle1@aol.com

For a catalog or more information on products by Rebecca Carter, please contact:

Designs by Rebecca
P.O. Box 1295
Bountiful, UT 84011-1295
Phone: (801) 292-6624
FAX: (801) 423-3219
e-mail:
    designsbyrebecca@uswest.net

Images on pages 96, 97, and 106 Copyright © 1996, 1998 PhotoDisc Inc.

About the Author

Rebecca Carter was born and raised in Bountiful, Utah. She currently resides in Salem, Utah with her husband Rick and her four children, Rachel, Tyrel, Chantry, and Sophie.

Rebecca is a graduate of Southern Utah State University, where she majored in fine arts and earned a three-year degree in interior design.

She has designed and marketed a hand-painted gift line for the decorative painter for the past eight years and now spends her time designing fabrics, craft books, stamps, greeting cards, and a gift line by Center Street Designs.

Dedication

To my children who stand by me each day and to my husband who is my best friend. Thank you for each memory and for the smiles and laughter that I see through the lens of the camera.

Acknowledgments

I would like to recognize the endless support my family has given me and thank them for standing by me through each new project I begin. This was a fun and new project for me and was a nice break from drawing and painting. My children were excited to work along side me and especially loved going to the scrapbook supply store to pick up those few missed items. Our basket was always filled with far more than what was on our list. You can never have too much card stock, die-cuts, or stickers.

I have loved photography for as long as I can remember. Sifting through boxes of photos is one of my favorite things to do. Laughing at childhood photos of friends and family brings the past to life once again. Nothing stimulates a child's mind as much as a childhood photo of a parent or grandparent. The questions begin and the memories flow.

I am grateful for the black-and-white photo my oldest brother, Dan, took of my younger brother, Paul. For some reason that photo has remained in my mind for 20 years. There is something about the effect of a black-and-white photo and the mood it sets. I have literally taken more than 100 black-and-white photos over the last few months of my children who have been so patient. They anxiously ask me, "When will you get them back?"

I would also like to thank the children in our neighborhood for letting me take endless pictures of them for holiday gift giving—you made my holiday that much brighter! You make our neighborhood complete with laughter and smiles and fill my children's lives with sweet memories.

Thanks to all of you! *Rebecca*

Table of Contents

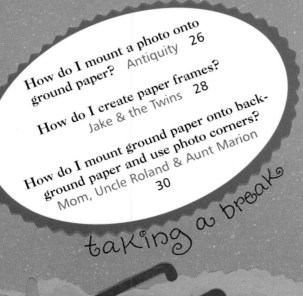

taking a break

digging for sand dollars

We buried Jake

Scrapbooking for the first time

Introduction

"Scrapbooking" is a hobby that not only provides a creative outlet for the scrapbook designer, but also promotes a strong sense of self-esteem and belonging for those whose lives and accomplishments are creatively chronicled and compiled into an album or collection of albums.

Great scrapbooks start with great photos. Although professional photos are wonderful additions to a scrapbook, using a professional photographer for all photos is not practical, or necessary. Your own snapshots are going to capture the most memorable moments in life.

The best times and conditions, as far as lighting is concerned, for taking photographs outside are before 10 am and after 4 pm and on a slightly overcast day. The subject should be positioned so the sunlight is hitting them from the side instead of facing directly into the sun.

Add variety to photos by changing the angles at which photos are taken. Try looking through the camera viewfinder at the subject from low, high, and normal camera angles to see which will look best. Children's photos are often better if the photographer kneels down to the child's level before taking the shot. Many older people find photos taken from a slightly higher angle more appealing.

Get closer to the subject when you are taking the photograph. The one comment I hear most often is, "Your pictures are so close-up! In my photos the people are always so far away." At first, it is a little awkward to get so close, but the results are great. The only exception to using this technique is when you are using a flash—especially indoors—as the subject can appear washed out or over-exposed.

Try enlarging your photos. If you have a photo where the image is very small and you would like it to appear larger, either enlarge it on a color copy machine or have the photo printed larger from the negative. Then simply crop the photo so the subject is the main focus.

Good photos come from good photo processing labs. Avoid the temptation to save money by going with a lower-quality lab. Incorrect developing can mean the difference between a photo that lasts and a photo that quickly fades.

Use both black-and-white and colored photos in your scrapbooks. While black-and-white photos last longer, the value of colored photos cannot be denied. Many scrapbook designers recommend taking colored photos for the most part and taking a set of black-and-white photos every six months to one year to preserve family history, in the event that color photos deteriorate.

Keep duplicates of favorite photos and negatives somewhere besides in the home. In the event of a fire, flood, or other natural disaster, at least some photos will survive. Duplicates can be kept with family, friends, or in a bank safe deposit box.

Many photos suggest a theme or represent a special event. For example, a photo of a child blowing out candles on a birthday cake can be used to build a page with a birthday theme. Decide what emotion or mood is reflected by the theme and use it as a guide when choosing paper patterns and accents.

Add color to scrapbook pages by using colored paper products, pens, markers, and more. You may choose to use colors that traditionally represent the theme of the scrapbook page or colors that are complementary to the colors found in the photos. Choose colors that reinforce and enhance the page's theme, not detract from it.

Use a few of the many available scrapbook supplies to accentuate the photos, theme, and colors.

As acid damages photos, it is important to use acid-free supplies when creating scrapbook pages. Scrapbook suppliers and most standard craft stores are great sources for papers, stickers, die-cuts, pens, and other acid-free products.

When you have pages that face each other, try to use complementary or coordinating colors and themes. Your scrapbook will appear neat and organized, not cluttered and hard to follow.

How to Use this Book

For the person who is scrapbooking for the first time, this book provides a comprehensive guide to products, supplies, and techniques that can be used to creatively compile these treasured histories.

Section 1 familiarizes you with the basic tools and supplies you need to begin scrapbooking. Section 2 begins with the most basic technique—how to mount a photo to the page. The second technique builds upon what you have already learned, adding a paper frame to the photo. Each subsequent technique continues in this manner, introducing a new technique and building on the last. If you decide to jump ahead out of sequence, you may find you have skipped a technique you now need to use.

Section 3 introduces new ideas and a few new products, but all use the previously learned techniques.

Finally, Section 4 provides a gallery of ideas, full of scrapbook pages that have been created by artists and professionals in the field.

The intent of this book is to provide a starting point and teach basic skills. The more pages you create, the more comfortable you will feel. Take pride in the talents you are developing and try to resist comparing your pages to any one else's. Everyone has their own style. Remember, the main idea is to get the photos into a photo album—not to have the best looking page in the neighborhood. Happy scrapbooking!

Section 1: *scrapbooking basics*

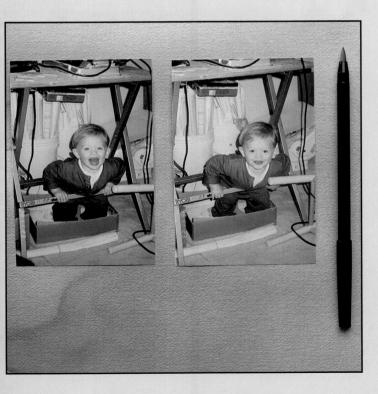

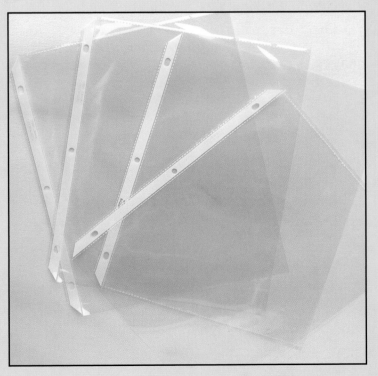

What do I need to get started?

Getting Started

Scrapbooking can be an overwhelming project if it is not broken down into categories. When I first began scrapbooking a few years ago, I bought everything in sight just because it was there, "Oh, that's cute," and "I must need that." From every store I went into, I came out with bags of "stuff" with no plan in mind. The kids and I sat down with boxes of photos and bags of stuff and in no time at all we had a big mess and only one page done. It was not fun.

Being organized has got to be the first priority on the list before beginning.

Organize Your Space

Arrange a place or even designate a "spot" where your supplies and photos are going to be stored. If at all possible, set up a table that can be left up with all of the supplies at hand. This will save time in having to gather the supplies and photos each time you would like to work on a page.

Organize Your Memories

Wash hands thoroughly before handling photos. Natural oils from skin can be harmful to photos, so even clean hands must be washed frequently while working on scrapbooks. When possible, try to handle photos by the edges or wear lightweight gloves.

When you receive the photos back from developing, discard any photos that are out of focus—a blank wall or the back of someone's head. Take a moment to identify the who, what, where, when, how, and why of each photo. Then, later, when you are ready to create the scrapbook page, the memories and thoughts will be fresh in your mind and it will make journaling easier. Write the information on the back or top edges of the photo, using a photo safe labeling pencil.

Many varieties of labeling pencils can be used to safely write on both front or back of a photo and will wipe off with a tissue. Do not use a ballpoint, felt tip, or water-based pen to label photos. These pens may create indentation lines on the photo's face and their inks may eventually bleed through, becoming visible on the face of the photo.

Next, sort these and any other photos and memorabilia that you may already have sitting in that drawer or shoe box. Obtain a box for each member of your family. I suggest a larger box to hold memorabilia, drawings, and special school papers; and another box specifically for photos. These boxes should be acid-free. There are many styles available and they are just the right size to protect the photos. Label the boxes either by the year or by the event.

Employ the knowledge of friends and family members to help identify dates, people, places, and events pictured (a family reunion or gathering is a good place to find such help).

This will take a bit of time, but once they are organized, the photos and momentos will be easily found and the craft of scrapbooking will be a positive experience instead of a headache.

Organize Your Supplies

Here is a list of basic supplies you will need to get started:

Adhesives (acid-free)
Card stock (acid-free)
Photo album
Photo corners
Photo safe pencil
Scissors
Sheet protectors (acid-free) (optional)
Templates
Transparent ruler

Adhesives: There are several different types of adhesives for mounting photos, ground paper, die-cuts, etc. When choosing any adhesive, make certain it is acid-free and photo-safe.

The adhesive a scrapbooker chooses is a personal preference. Some of the different products available are:

Glue stick—This is a basic glue that you may already have at home. It is clean and easy to use. It works well for mounting die-cuts and punch-outs.

Mounting tape—This adhesive is best to use for mounting a photo onto a prefinished photo matte.

Photo sticker squares—Although these double-sided tape squares were developed for adhering a photo, they can be used to adhere just about anything. These are quick and easy.

Wet bond—This is a liquid glue that is available with a jumbo tip for larger coverage or a pencil tip for smaller projects.

Card Stock: Acid-free colored card stock is one of my favorite items to use on a page because it adds color and dimension without detracting from the photos. It is inexpensive and, by adding the effect of a few different decorative-edged scissors, a thousand layouts can be created. Card stock comes in hundreds of colors, textures, and weights. Be certain to familiarize yourself with the product available.

Card stock is the most widely used paper for scrapbooking and comes in lightweight, medium weight, and heavy weight (sometimes referred to as cover weight). Decide which weight works best for your purposes. Here are a few characteristics to consider:

Lightweight card stock—Choose this weight when you want to use decorative-edged scissors and craft punches, as it leaves a very clean edge. Lightweight card stock is not the best for the ground or background sheet, as it tends to be flimsy once photos are mounted onto it.

Medium-weight card stock—This weight is the most widely used as it is acts well as a ground paper and also is easy to cut with decorative-edged scissors and craft punches.

Heavy-weight card stock—I like to use this weight whenever possible for the ground or background paper, making the page very sturdy. Avoid using this weight when using decorative-edged scissors or punches. The thickness of the paper wears the blades and results in unclean cuts.

Photo Album: Albums and binders are available in all sizes, colors, styles, and formats. The main difference between scrapbooks is in the binding. Album bindings should allow pages to lie flat. Choose from three-ring binders, expandable binders, and bound scrapbooks.

Take some time to decide the size of album you want to use. The 12" x 12" format allows more space to arrange the photos, whereas there may be a larger assortment of stationery and decorative papers available in the 8½" x 11" format.

One approach may be to have at least one album for each family member and another to represent the entire family. Choose a scrapbook album that allows for the greatest amount of flexibility and creativity.

Photo Corners: Photo corners have been used for many years to secure photos on a page without adhering the photo itself. Today, photo corners are available in a variety of styles and colors from transparent to gold and silver.

Decorative photo corners—These photo corners are laser-cut and come flat in a sheet. They need to be folded and assembled and require the use of an adhesive, but they are well worth the time.

Mounting corners—These photo corners are available in a wide range of colors. They are made of heavy paper and must be moistened to adhere onto the page.

Transparent photo corners—These photo corners are self-adhesive. They are designed to hold a photo without detracting from the photo.

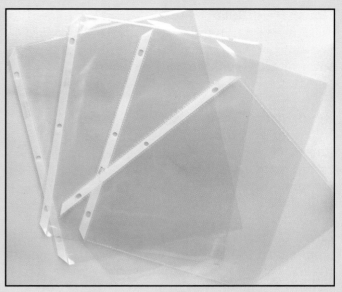

Photo Safe Labeling Pencil: A photo labeling pencil should be used for recording information about the photo and for tracing a stencil or template to a photo.

Scissors: It is important to have a good sharp pair of scissors to ensure clean lines. I prefer to use the type that has a spring in the handle which makes it so your hand does not get tired when cutting for a long time. The spring makes it very easy when cutting around shapes—especially ovals and circles. I use a large pair for general cutting and a small pair for small intricate cuts.

Sheet Protectors: Sheet protectors envelope the scrapbook pages and keep photos on facing pages from rubbing together. They are available in both 12" x 12" and 8½" x 11" formats—for both the three-ring binder and the expandable binder pages. Sheet protectors come in different weights and finishes from nonglare to high-gloss. Choose one that you are comfortable working with and stay consistent from book to book.

Top-loading sheet protectors—These are available in both 12" x 12" and 8½" x 11" formats.

Templates: Templates are used to crop photos and papers into shapes, such as hearts, circles, stars, balloons, etc., to eliminate unnecessary background or to match a theme.

Templates are available in a wide range of shapes and sizes. Transparent templates are useful for exact placement of the design. Cookie cutters also work well as templates

Position templates over item to be trimmed, trace shape, and cut out. Use a photo safe labeling pencil when tracing to a photo as any remnant tracing will wipe off with a tissue.

Transparent Ruler: I use a transparent ruler on almost every page I create. Getting straight lines and making certain the photo is adhered straight are very important on a scrapbook page, and this ruler makes it easy to achieve both.

Beyond the Basic Supplies

As interest grows, so will a collection of fun-to-have supplies. The following is a listing of the many available supplies that I would recommend for quick and easy ways to complete your pages.

Circle Cutter: This tool adjusts to the desired diameter of the circle. It makes a perfectly clean circular cut. The circle cutter is great when a template does not have the exact size of circle you may need.

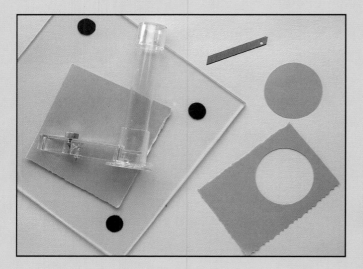

Clip-art: Lined art images are available in booklets to copy and cut to accent scrapbook pages. Clip-art is also available in the form of computer software and can be printed to paper and cut out for quick and easy page decorations.

Color Wheel: This tool is a visual representation of the spectrum of colors in the shape of a wheel. When choosing colors, select a primary color and use the wheel to choose complementary colors.

Corner Rounders: These are similar in appearance to craft punches. They trim square corners off photos and papers, leaving curved corners.

Corner Templates: These are used to trim corners on photos and papers into shapes. Position clear acrylic templates over item to be trimmed, trace shape, and cut. Use a photo labeling pencil when tracing to a photo as any remnant tracing will wipe off with a tissue.

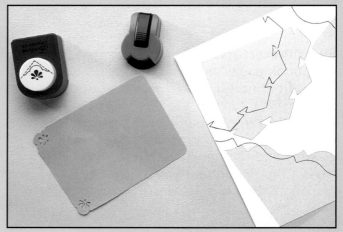

Craft Knife: A knife with a replaceable blade makes cutting straight edges and tight corners clean and easy.

Craft Punches: These are available in several sizes and motifs, from hearts to dinosaurs, stars to palm trees, and more. These are used to punch colored paper or card stock for small shapes to enhance a page.

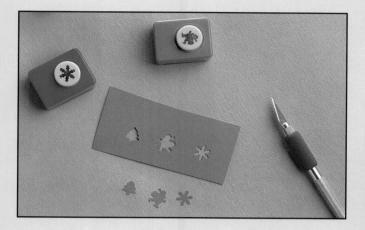

Crimper: A crimper corrugates papers and cards, adding dimension and texture to a page.

Decorative-edged Scissors: Use these fun scissors to cut paper with distinctive edges. There are several different edges to choose from to accent any theme.

Avoid cutting photos with decorative-edged scissors. These scissors are primarily for cutting and trimming card stock.

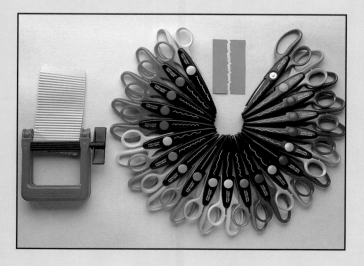

Die-cuts: Die-cuts are available in several colors and sizes. They are cut from varied weights of paper and are a quick way to add thematic shapes and colors to a page. Die-cuts can be purchased individually or in theme packets. Many paper stores have a die-cut machine that patrons can use to cut their own papers, to get both the shape and color they desire.

Embossing Stencils: These brass plates are available in several designs that can be gently pressed into scrapbook papers, creating a raised effect.

Lettering Booklets: Learn creative techniques of writing and decorating the alphabet. These booklets demonstrate how to complete styles, such as dot, outline, and block lettering. Refer to photo on page 18.

Light Box: Available in varied sizes, these boxes have an acrylic top and a light enclosed within. Use them to transfer clip-art or lettering designs directly to the ground paper or paper label. Place the design, right side up, on a light box and the ground paper or paper label on top, right side up. Trace the design to the paper. Note: This technique can be duplicated by holding the design and ground paper or paper label up to a sunlit window. Refer to photo on page 18.

Paper Cutter: A good compact paper cutter is a nice addition to your tools. It will cut the 12" x 12" paper, extend out to 15" for measuring left- or right-handed, and has an inexpensive replaceable blade. I often use this to cut ground paper and trim photos.

Novelty-edged Rulers: These rulers are used to create a continuous pattern along one or more edges of a paper. Patterns include wavy, zigzag, scallop, and more. Position clear acrylic rulers on paper, trace pattern, and cut.

Paper: Add dimension and color to a scrapbook with paper. Card stock (mentioned on page 13) is a heavier weight paper often used as a ground paper or for creating die-cuts. Decorative or novelty papers and stationery are often used for page backgrounds and to create patterns and borders.

Pens, Pencils & Markers: Use these for labeling, highlighting, and journaling. Make certain pens and markers are fade-proof, waterproof, and use pigment ink. Pens and markers are available in all colors and with several different tips, such as .01 tip for creating fine lines, and tiny accents; .05 tip for standard clean lines; and a 45° angle for calligraphic effect for titles and special emphasis. Colored pencils that are water-resistant and light-fast can also be used to decorate scrapbook pages.

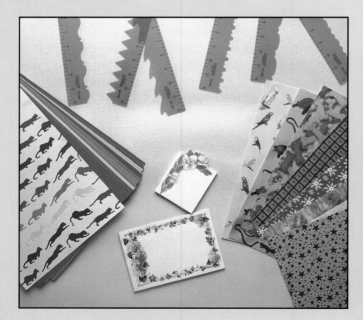

pH Testing Pen: This amazing pen instantly tests acid content of paper.

Premade Photo Mattes: These are available in several colors. Embossed and of card stock thickness, these can be used to matte studio portrait photos.

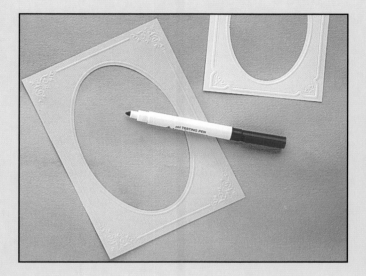

Red Eye Pen: This pen fixes red eyes on photos. It contains a dye that filters out the color red, allowing natural eye features to show through.

Rubber Stamps, Pigment Ink Pads, Embossing Powder & Heat Tool: There are numerous individual rubber stamps, rubber stamp kits, and pigment ink pads available to use to enhance a scrapbook page. After stamping, color in the designs with pigment ink brush markers and/or apply colored embossing powder and heat-set with a heat tool.

Stickers: Stickers are available in all sorts of themes, sizes, and colors. They add instant artistic impact, or color, or humor.

Organize Your Storage

Once you have collected a few basic supplies, store them in a safe place. Shoe boxes with lids work great for storing adhesives, craft punches, and scissors.

Tools such as these can also be stored in clear, plastic, stackable drawers. Portable canvas bags with multiple pockets also prove useful for storing and carrying needed supplies.

Keep items such as stickers, die cut shapes, punch shapes, papers, and scraps either in zipper-type baggies with holes punched along one side of the bags, or in clear 2" x 2" slide size, 3½" x 2" sports card size, 4" x 6" photo size, or 8½" x 11" top-loading protector sheets. Organize them by occasion and color and store them together in a 3-ring binder.

I believe it is important to keep your supplies handy and in a safe place, so the time you spend scrapbooking is time spent creating instead of searching for the lost scissors or glue sticks.

Creating Scrapbook Pages

Once you have gathered and organized your supplies, you are ready to begin creating pages. Here are a few tips for a smooth start.

Sharing Costs

Sharing the expense can really ease the cost of scrapbooking supplies. If a group of friends gets together on the cost of some supplies, such as the decorative-edged scissors and craft punches, you will all have a larger variety of products to create with. Also, there is such a large number of styles of scissors—where do you start? Before you make a large purchase, start with the basics and share the others.

Color-copying Photos

One important tool you may want to consider is a laser or color copier. Copy the photo that seems to be missing its negative or an older photo of parents or grandparents. The laser copier is so advanced that you can make a copy of an old black-and-white photo and mount it onto a page. Black-and-whites are so important to have in photo albums. I have made many laser copies of old photos, framed the copies, and shared them as Christmas presents. What a treat!

Finding a Starting Point

Start where you feel the most comfortable. This may be designing a page for last month's birthday or last year's Christmas celebration. The idea is to just start. Once your first few pages are complete, the rest will become very easy.

Layout

For each page, choose two to four photos. Be selective when choosing and mounting photos. They should be well-focused, interesting, and varied.

The layout of the pages seems to frighten people the most. In 90% of designs, the triangle rule is the easiest to follow. On pages that have more than one photo, place them in a triangle pattern. Refer to examples below.

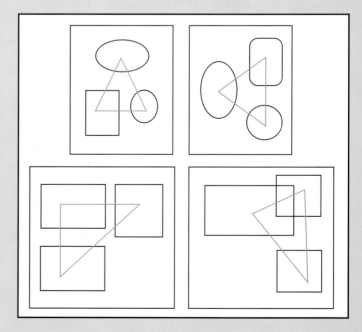

The placement of stickers, die-cuts, and memorabilia can also follow this same rule. After practicing this rule on a few pages you will find it easier to do. The pages are more pleasing to the eye because they are balanced.

Finding Balance

Do not feel like every inch of the paper needs to be filled up with stickers or lettering. A very simple rule to follow is, "Less is sometimes better." Remember that the photo is supposed to be the main focus, not the sticker or the printed ground paper. Leave some empty areas, or negative space, and you will find that these are much more appealing pages to look at.

There are some pages that lend themselves to a lot of stuff. Refer to "Life as a Teen" on page 76. This page is purposely filled to capacity because of the intent. However, you should keep these pages few and far between.

Scrapbooking Terms

Sometimes it seems as if scrapbookers speak their own language. The following listing of common terms will help you feel comfortable when you visit the local scrapbook store.

Adhere: Adhering is the actual process of mounting the item or photo, using mounting strips, glue, or photo corners.

Background Paper: Background paper is the paper used as a border onto which the ground paper is adhered or mounted.

Crop: This term is often used to refer to a gathering of friends on a set date at a set time and place to work together on individual scrapbooks and share supplies and ideas for pages. Scrapbookers often plan monthly get-togethers that last for several hours and include potluck-style refreshments. The crop can be held in a scrapbooker's home or in a larger facility, such as a church building. Sometimes a crop is the main event in a getaway weekend with family or friends.

Cropping Photos: Many scrapbook designers will choose to crop, or cut, photos to remove unwanted background, emphasizing the foreground or people, and to create fun shapes. Snapshots, which are often incorrectly framed at the time of photographing the subject, are candidates for cropping. This technique will not affect the stability of a photo. Cropping is completely safe, but it is irreversible. Consider cropping color copies of irreplaceable one-of-a-kind photos.

Cropping studio photos is not recommended, since professional photos are typically framed well, with little unnecessary background. Studio portraits can be framed with decorative paper cutouts or premade photo mattes. NEVER crop an instant photo. Make color copies of instant photos. The color copies can then be cropped as desired and added to pages.

Ground Paper: Ground paper is that onto which the photos are adhered or mounted.

Journaling: Journaling is documenting photos by either hand-writing or lettering names, dates, and events—again, the who, what, where, when, how, and why—on the ground paper. Write personal feelings and humorous captions about the event. Include family stories, poems, and songs that correspond with the photo. For a child's scrapbook, write down first words, favorite phrases, and any grammatical errors and manners of speech to capture the child's development over time.

When adding a journal entry that is quite lengthy, type it or use a computer to avoid making mistakes that would cause you to have to start again.

Lettering: Lettering is the technique of creatively writing and decorating words, phrases, and titles. This technique makes the text an element of page design, drawing attention to the words. There are many different styles to choose from. Write the words in the lettering style on the page in pencil first, then go over pencil with a pen or marker.

Memorabilia: The purpose of creating a scrapbook is to provide a place to keep "scraps!" Tangible reminders of people, places, and events can include any of the following memorabilia.

Announcements
Awards
Birth certificates, hospital bracelets, sonogram copies, etc.
Brochures
Certificates
Children's drawings
Greeting cards
Handprints
Letters
Locks of hair
Maps
Marriage licenses
Menus
Newspaper clippings
Obituaries
Post cards
Programs
Report cards
Ribbons
Ticket stubs
Wedding invitations

Make certain to use page protectors to keep these momentos in place.

Pocket Pages: To hold memorabilia separate from a photo page, create a pocket page by gluing two ground papers together along bottom and both sides. Remember to cut a curve into the top edge of the top page for easy access to the contents of the pocket page.

Creating an Archival-quality Scrapbook

Many scrapbookers want their scrapbooks to be archival, or able to stand the test of time. The primary enemy to this goal is acid.

An object that has a pH less than 7.0 is said to have acid, an unstable chemical substance that will weaken paper and photos, leading to yellowing and brittleness. Items kept in a scrapbook or used to decorate the pages should be acid-free or have a pH of 7.0 or more.

When shopping for paper for pages, choose acid-free, lignin-free papers which have had acid removed from the manufacturing process or have been treated to neutralize acids.

Buffered paper, which is not only acid-free, but is also acid-absorbent. Buffered paper has added calcium carbonate that will absorb acid that may come into contact with the paper. Many designers will use buffered paper at the front and back of a scrapbook to protect pages from gasses or acids given off by the binder.

Archival-quality paper may be slightly more expensive, but the expense is worthwhile. Scrapbooks made with low-quality, highly acidic papers will fade and tear over time. Low-quality paper may even irreversibly damage the very photos a scrapbook is intended to protect.

Scrapbook suppliers also sell acid-free stickers, cards, photo corners, and pens to complement acid-free background paper and photos. Permanent pigment pens are the best, since their colors last longer and are less likely to run or smear over time. Read the label on any pen, or call the manufacturer's customer service line if the label does not indicate if the pen is acid-free.

Although a product may start out acid-free, there is no guarantee it will stay that way. Acid can move into the product from other high-acid objects in close contact, from environmental pollutants, or even from contact with oils in human hands. Acid from high-acid products will always migrate to acid-free products.

Do not use crepe paper or construction paper in a scrap book. These papers will fade and tear quickly, and their colors may bleed onto photos.

Remember, never place photos in a "magnetic page" self-adhesive photo album. Self-adhesive albums are covered in polyvinyl chloride (PVC), a plastic that releases hydrochloric acid. Acids will actually eat away at pictures, causing them to become yellow and brittle. To make matters worse, the adhesives in these albums will absorb into photos over time, making them difficult, if not impossible, to remove.

Adhesives used for scrapbooks can also be a source of potential damage. Do not use regular transparent tape, high-acid rubber cement, super glue, or high-acid craft glue in a scrapbook. There are several acid-free adhesives on the market. Carefully read product labels to make certain adhesives are acid-free before using them. If there is a question, call the product customer service line.

Truly archival-quality scrapbooks should be reversible. This means that photos placed in the scrapbook can be taken out again with no resulting damage. To make this possible, a scrapbook designer would need to use either a removable adhesive, or photo corners to secure photos.

Don'ts

The following items and practices should be avoided when compiling scrapbooks:

Ballpoint pen on photos
Construction and crepe paper
Cropping instant photos
Cropping very old or priceless photos
Exposing scrapbooks to water, exhaust, humidity, insects, extreme heat, or direct light
Felt-tip and water-based pens
Fingerprints on photos
Magnetic self-adhesive photo albums and pages
Masking tape
PVC plastic pages
Rubber cement
Storing scrapbooks and photo negatives in the same location
Transparent tape

Important Reminders

Do not forget to "journal" on your pages. The photos are visually interesting, but reading about the story behind the photos is necessary for future generations. Consider inserting actual journal pages into the album every so often. Children's words to a conversation or prayer are always wonderful to read about later—especially for the child as he or she grows older.

Keep in mind the true purpose to putting together a scrapbook—getting the photos into a safe, dry place. If your interest does not include adding stickers, die-cuts, etc., concentrate on mounting and labeling the photos. Protect the memories that can easily fade.

← my cake!

May 19th 1998

Spencer

Braden

Jake

We had my party in our front yard. It was sooo windy!! I had a dinosaur cake and got a lot of dinosaur toys! It was so much fun!

Abby

← the can was empty!

then there are those who like to watch!

Barb

The camp site

Sophie

Sophie was finding all sorts of treasures!!

What a fun Halloween! We had purchased these teeth from a friend of ours and Ty, Rachel & Dad had a ball! The scary thing was... Rick fit into the character a little too well. Rachel & her friend, Jennifer laughed the whole time she was getting dressed, adding crooked pigtails, lipstick & tissue from her long-johns. Ty was a true hillbilly. He & his friend Christopher were gone for hours & came home with bags of candy. ♥ Sophie & Chantry were just your cute, normal halloween kids. They traveled the neighborhood with Dad but once home, Sophie squealed each time the door bell rang, running with candy in hand to fill the bags. We all are excited for next year... oh.. what will we be? Come see!!

Section 2: *techniques*

1 technique

How do I mount a photo onto ground paper?

What You Need to Get Started:

2 photos per page
Adhesive
Card stock:
   brown for
   ground paper
Pencil

Start out simple when beginning to scrapbook. The main idea and focus is to get the photos into an album to protect them, instead of being piled into a box "somewhere" in the basement. Some of us prefer this simple style where the photos are nicely displayed on a page without a lot of decoration.

Antiquity

Here's How:

1. Arrange the photos on the ground paper as desired.

2. Using the pencil, lightly mark around the corners of the photos.

3. Remove the photos from the ground paper.

4. Beginning with the photos that are closest to the ground paper (if your photos overlap), apply adhesive to the back of each photo. Adhere them onto the ground paper, as marked, one at a time.

Troubleshooting:

Look for adhesives that are acid-free or that are labeled photo safe, meaning that the manufacturer has taken extra steps to ensure that the adhesive is free of materials that might damage the photo.

Avoid adhesives that emit odors or fumes. This is often a sign that the adhesive contains elements which can damage the photo.

Design Tip:

Experiment with different types of adhesives to find those that will make scrapbbooking easy and fun for you. There is such a wide variety to choose from—permanent or temporary, pen or stick, tape or tabs.

2 technique

How do I create paper frames?

Placing a paper frame behind a photo gives it a finished look. Hold your photo next to several different colors of card stock to determine which color will best complement the image. Choose a contrasting ground paper so the paper frame stands out against the background.

Jake & the Twins

Here's How:
1. Apply adhesive to the back of each photo. Adhere them onto ivory card stock, allowing enough space around the entire photo for a paper "frame."

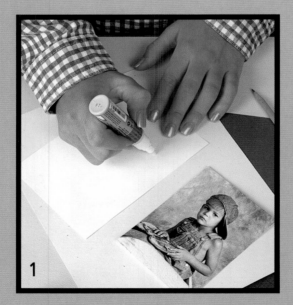

3. Refer to Technique 1 on page 26. Arrange and adhere the photos onto the ground paper.

2. Using scissors, cut the card stock ⅜" larger than the large photos all around and ¼" larger than the smaller photos all around.

**What You Need
to Get Started:**

1 photo per page
Adhesive
Card stock:
  olive green
  speckled for
  ground paper
Decorative
  border: light
  brown with
  vine design
Decorative paper:
  vine print for
  background
  paper
Decorative photo
  corners: light
  brown with
  vine design
Paper cutter
Pencil
Scissors
Transparent ruler

How do I mount ground paper onto background paper and use photo corners?

Photo corners are mostly for photos that you may not want permanently mounted in the photo album. Photos can be easily removed and used for other purposes. Some photo corners are self-adhesive while others may require the use of an adhesive to adhere them to the scrapbook page.

Mom, Uncle Roland & Aunt Marion

Here's How:

1. Using the pencil, transparent ruler, and paper cutter, measure, mark, and cut ¾" off of the bottom and one side of the ground paper.

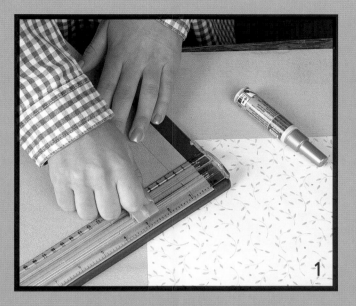

2. Apply adhesive to the back of the ground paper. Adhere it onto the center of the background paper, creating a ⅜" border.

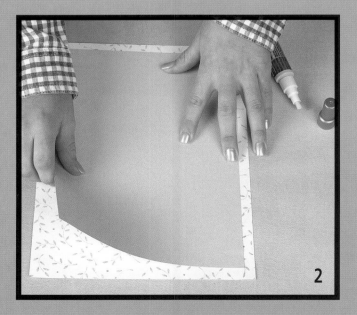

3. Arrange the photo on the ground paper as desired. Apply adhesive to the back of the decorative photo corner. Hold the photo in place with one hand and carefully slide a corner over the photo, adhering it onto the ground paper. Repeat for the opposite corner and then the two remaining corners.

4. Using the scissors, trim the decorative border to fit the width of the ground paper. Apply adhesive to the back of the decorative border. Adhere it onto the ground paper.

Design Tips:

Depending on the type of photo corners you choose, there are a couple of different ways of adhering the corners onto the ground paper. Refer to Photos Corners on page 14 for options.

If the decorative photo corners are being used as decorative elements, apply photo sticker squares to the backs of the corners and adhere them onto the sides of the photo instead of at the corners.

technique 4

How do I use premade photo mattes on a printed ground paper?

What You Need to Get Started:

2 photos per page
Adhesive
Decorative paper: rose print for ground paper
Marker: 0.5 mm black liner
Paper labels
Premade photo mattes to fit photos
Tape

Premade photo mattes are prefect for framing professional studio photos. They are cut to a standard size, which makes centering the photos very easy. Most mattes have embossed designs that add texture but do not take away from the image in the photo. Because the mattes are a solid color, they balance out a printed background that may otherwise be too heavy or overpowering.

Sophia

Here's How:

1. Place premade photo mattes face down on the work surface. Center each photo face down on the matte.

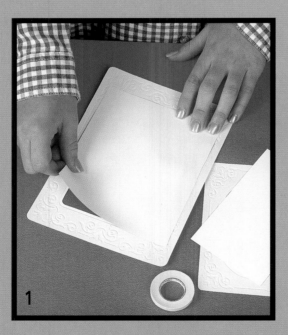

3. Using the marker, add journaling to the paper labels.

4. Refer to Technique 1 on page 26. Arrange and adhere the matted photos and paper labels onto the ground paper.

2. Place tape on the sides of the photo matte and adhere the photo.

Design Tips:

It is easier to tape the photo behind the frame, and then adhere the frame onto the background. It is much more difficult if you try to adhere the photo and then the frame. Avoid mistakes by centering the photo correctly before adhering it onto either the matte or the ground paper.

33

5 technique

How do I use decorative-edged scissors?

Decorative-edged scissors are a wonderful way to dress up any paper frame or paper border. Most of these scissors will cut two different designs depending on how you hold them in your hand. Choose the edge that will best complement the photo or theme. Never use the decorative-edged scissors on the photo, as it detracts from the photo.

Easter Bunnies

Here's How:

1. Using the pencil, transparent ruler, and paper cutter, measure, mark, and cut ½" off the top and one side of the ground paper.

2. Position the cloud decorative-edged scissors in your hand so the desired edge will cut. Trim all sides of the ground paper, matching up the edge design with each cut of the scissors.

3. Apply adhesive to the back of the ground paper. Adhere it onto the center of the background paper.

4. Refer to Technique 3 on page 30. Arrange and adhere the photos and the decorative photo corners onto the light blue, lavender, and pink card stock, allowing enough space around the photo for creating a paper "frame."

5. Refer to Technique 2 on page 28. Using decorative-edged scissors, cut the card stock ¼" larger than the photo all around.

6. Apply adhesive to the back of the paper label. Adhere it onto the light green card stock. Using decorative-edged scissors, cut card stock ⅛" larger than the paper label all around.

7. Using the markers, add journaling to the paper label.

8. Refer to Technique 1 on page 26. Arrange and adhere each framed photo and the paper label onto the ground paper.

Easter 1994

How do I use a template to crop photos?

What You Need to Get Started:

2 photos per page
Adhesive
Card stock: olive green speckled; sage green speckled; ivory; tan parchment for background paper; tan speckled for ground paper
Decorative-edged scissors: stamp
Markers: 0.5 mm black liner; 1.2 mm black liner
Paper cutter
Pencil: soft lead
Scissors
Templates: oval; rectangle
Transparent ruler

Cropping becomes necessary when there is a lot of wasted space around the image on which you are focusing. Crop out the undesirable portions to make the most of your photo.

My Dad's Old Hat

Here's How:

1. Using the pencil, transparent ruler, and paper cutter, measure, mark, and cut ½" off the top and one side of the ground paper.

2. Using the decorative-edged scissors, trim all sides of the ground paper.

3. Apply adhesive to the back of the ground paper. Adhere it onto the center of the background paper, creating a ⅜" border.

4. To crop each photo, place the template over the photo to the best position. Using the pencil, trace the shape onto the photo.

5. Using scissors, cut around the pencil line on each photo. For a smooth cutting line, follow these steps:

• If you are right-handed, hold the photo in your left hand then, with your right hand, open the scissors all the way. Place the photo to the inside "v" of the scissors.

• Make the cut, using all but ¾" from the tip of the blade before opening the scissors again.

• Use long smooth cuts instead of short choppy ones and turn or guide the photo with your left hand not with the scissors.

• Do not cut all the way to the tip of the scissors in the middle of a shape as the paper tends to split.

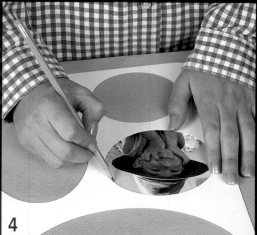

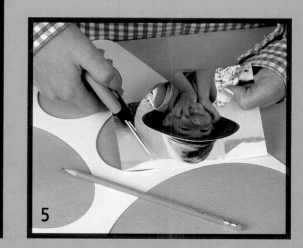

6. Refer to Technique 2 on page 28. Adhere corresponding photos onto the coordinating card stock. Cut the card stock ⅜" larger than the photo all around.

7. Using the decorative-edged scissors, cut a 6¼" x 1¼" piece of ivory card stock. Adhere the ivory card stock onto the sage green card stock. Using scissors, cut the sage green card stock ½" larger than the ivory card stock all around.

8. Using the 0.5 mm marker, add journaling to the ivory card stock.

9. Apply adhesive to the back of the sage green card stock. Adhere it onto the ground paper, centered from side to side and ¼" from the bottom.

10. Refer to Technique 1 on page 26. Arrange and adhere the photos onto the ground paper.

11. Using the 1.2 mm marker, add journaling to the ground paper near the photos.

Design Tips:

The children were the focal point in the upper photo, but the excessive background was detracting. Cropping the image brought the focus back to the children and actually made them appear larger.

In the bottom photo, cropping in tight on the child, and using an oval shape to accentuate the hat, gave me the "close up" effect that I was looking for.

Practice first before tracing a template and cutting original photos. If this is your first time cropping a photo or cutting

around corners and ovals, I suggest making color copies of some photos and using them to practice cropping and cutting.

Ovals are the hardest shape to cut. You want smooth cuts—not jagged edges or straight cuts where the line begins to curve. It is better to have a pile of practice sheets instead of a pile of photos that are cropped and cut not to your liking.

Use different sizes and shapes of cropping templates to add interest to the page.

Hunter & Rylee
age 4
Spencer
age 4
Chantry
age 5

my,
dad's
old hat

My friends and I love to run and jump off the large rocks in my backyard. Spencer is wearing my dad's old hat and loves to have his picture taken. My mom took these pictures in October 1998.

How do I use corner punches and craft punches?

What You Need to Get Started:

1 photo per page
Adhesive
Card stock: navy
    blue for ground
    paper; cream;
    dark green;
    white
Corner rounder
    punch
Craft punch:
    snowflake
Markers: 0.5 mm
    blue liner;
    1.2 mm blue
    liner
Pencil
Scissors
Transparent ruler

The corner rounder is perfect for rounding the corners of the photo instead of using scissors. The tool is easy to use and all of the corners will match. One simple way to enhance a page is by punching a motif from corners and edges. Use the punched out images for added design around the page.

Best Buddies

Here's How:
1. Using the corner rounder punch, insert the corner of the photo into the punch and round each corner.

2. Refer to Technique 2 on page 28. Adhere photo onto the dark green card stock. Cut the card stock ⅜" larger than the photo all around.

3. Using the snowflake punch, punch each corner of the of dark green card

stock. Note: When you are punching out motifs in the corners, it is hard to see the placement. Turn the punch upside down, slide the card stock in, and punch. The punch is harder to hold this way, but you can see the placement of the motif easier.

4. Apply adhesive to the back of the dark green card stock. Adhere it onto the cream card stock. Cut the cream card stock ¼" larger than the dark green card stock all around.

5. Apply adhesive to the back of the cream card stock. Adhere it onto the ground paper.

6. Refer to Technique 2 on page 28 to create a paper label. Using scissors, cut a 3¾" x 1¼" piece of white card stock. Apply adhesive to the back of the white card stock. Adhere it onto the dark green card stock. Cut the dark green card stock ⅛" larger than the white card stock all around. Adhere the dark green card stock onto the cream card stock. Cut the cream card stock ¼" larger than the dark green card stock all around. Using the corner rounder, round the corners of the cream card stock.

7. Using markers, add journaling to the paper label.

8. Apply adhesive to the back of the paper label. Adhere it onto the ground paper.

9. Using the snowflake punch, punch approximately 25 snowflakes from the white card stock.

10. Apply adhesive to the backs of the snowflakes. Randomly adhere them onto the ground paper and photo frame.

Troubleshooting:
The more intricate the craft punch, the more the blades will stick after punching. To release the button, press the dot of the design on the underside where the paper comes up, using a ballpoint pen.

Punch through waxed paper several times to lubricate the blades.

When the cuts from the punch are not very clean, punch through very fine sand paper several times to sharpen the blades.

Design Tip:
Overlap the punch designs onto the photo border. This will add some dimension.

" BEST BUDDIES "
Mason and Cody playing in their snow cave. February 2 '97

How do I use templates to embellish pages?

Most of the new templates have a decorative-edged border. This is a larger design not found on decorative-edged scissors. I like to use these templates to divide up larger areas of paper—like the 12" x 12" papers. The templates take a little more time to use, but add a bit more variety to the pages.

Sophie

Note: If this is your first time working with stencils, begin with a very simple edge and work up to more difficult lines. Refer to photo on page 25 for facing page layout.

Here's How:
1. Using the transparent ruler, pencil, and paper cutter, measure, mark, and cut 1" off one side of the ground paper. (If you are using 8½" x 11" paper, measure from the 8½" width.)

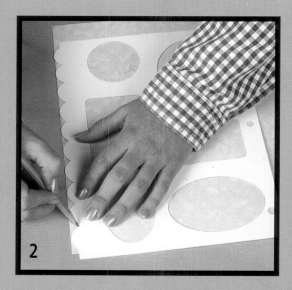

2. Place the scallop-edged template along the cut edge. Trace the design. Some of the decorative-edged templates may not be long enough to accommodate the 12" x 12" scrapbook pages. After tracing the design along the edge of your paper, slide the template up and continue the pattern.

3. Using scissors, carefully cut along traced line. Cut slowly to get nice smooth lines.

4. Cut a 1½" strip of white card stock that is the length of your page. Place the scallop-edged template along one

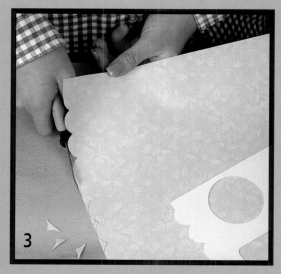

long edge and trace the design. Carefully cut along traced line.

5. Cut a 3" strip of background paper that is the length of your page.

6. Apply adhesive to the back of the ground paper along the scalloped edge only. Position the scalloped white card stock strip under the ground paper so about ⅛" of white is extending beyond the ground paper. Adhere them together.

7. Apply adhesive to the back of the white card stock strip along the scalloped edge only. Position the 3" strip of background paper under the ground paper and white card stock so the total width is equal to the total width of your page. Adhere them together.

8. Refer to Technique 6 on page 36. Using templates, a pencil, and scissors, crop selected photos as desired. Refer to Technique 7 on page 38. Round each corner of desired photos.

9. Refer to Technique 2 on page 28. Adhere photos onto the white card stock. Cut the card stock ¼" larger than the large photos and ⅛" larger than the smaller photos all around.

10. Using the cloud decorative-edged scissors, trim the edges of the journal entry paper. Adhere the journal entry paper onto the blue plaid paper. Using scissors, cut the blue plaid paper ½" larger than the journal entry paper all around.

11. Using the 1.2 mm liner marker, add journaling to the paper labels.

12. Refer to Technique 1 on page 26. Arrange and adhere the photos, journal entry, and paper labels onto the ground paper.

April 1998

Mom and Dad let Rachel and Tyrel decide on the Spring-break vacation. They decided on the Casa Blanca in Mesquite Nevada.

They HAD to buy me all new stuff from my levi hat to my flower sunglasses. I was all set to go.

It was the perfect weekend and we all had a great time especially in the pool which had a waterslide and a beautiful waterfall surrounded by flower gardens and palm trees. I loved to watch the kids come down the slide and splash water at me at the bottom.

I kept the hat on most of the time but the flower sunglasses were better just to chew on. That grass was a bit "prickly" and would rather sit on dad's lap and play with the camera.

9
technique

What You Need to Get Started:

3 photos per page
Adhesive
Card stock: blue; dark sage green; sage green; tan for ground paper; yellow
Die-cuts: cloud; flame; logs; mountains; tent
Markers: 0.5 mm black liner; 1.2 mm black liner
Opaque pens: blue; white
Pencil
Scissors
Templates: circle; oval; rectangle; square
Transparent ruler

How do I use die-cuts on a page?

This is an easy and inexpensive way to add design and color to a page. Die-cuts are ready-made and available in all colors, shapes, and sizes.

South Fork Canyon

Note: Refer to photo on page 24 for facing page layout.

Here's How:

1. Refer to Technique 6 on page 36. Crop selected photos as desired.

2. Refer to Technique 2 on page 28. Adhere selected photos onto assorted colors of card stock. Cut the colored card stock ¼" larger than the large photos and ⅛" larger than the smaller photos all around.

3. Refer to Technique 1 on page 26. Arrange and adhere the photos and die-cuts onto the ground paper.

4. Using the markers and opaque pens, add journaling to the die-cuts and ground paper.

Design Tip:

Do not be afraid to overlap the die-cuts with each other and also with the photos. Try using them as a background. Layering die-cuts and photos adds dimension to the pages.

How do I silhouette photos?

Silhouetting is perfect if you have a lot of photos of the same event. It is also great if there is a large group of people to show on the same layout.

What You Need to Get Started:

8–10 photos per page
Adhesive
Card stock:
  green; red;
  white for
  ground paper;
Craft knife and
  cutting mat
Decorative-edged
  scissors: cloud
Die-cuts: birthday
  cake; star
Markers: 0.5 mm
  black liner;
  1.2 mm black
  liner
Pencil
Scissors
Templates: oval;
  rectangle;
  square
Transparent ruler

I Am Five Today

Note: Make plenty of color copies for silhouettes so original photos are not ruined. Refer to photo on page 24 for facing page layout.

Here's How:

1. Using the transparent ruler, pencil, and cloud decorative-edged scissors, measure, mark, and cut ½" from the top and one side of the ground paper.

2. Apply adhesive to the back of the ground paper. Adhere it onto the of background paper, lining up the two uncut edges and leaving a colored border on the right and top edges. If you have a facing page, repeat with a second piece of ground paper and background paper, leaving a colored border on the left and top edges.

3. Refer to Technique 6 on page 36. Crop photos to be used at the top of the page as desired.

4. Refer to Technique 2 on page 28. Adhere one of the cropped photos onto green card stock. Cut the card stock ¼" larger than the photo all around.

5. Using a craft knife or scissors, carefully cut around the photographic or copied images to be used for silhouetting.

5

6. Arrange the blunt-edged silhouetted photos on the ground paper, lining them up along the bottom of the page, and placing them in varying heights, slightly overlapping them if necessary.

7. Arrange the cropped photos on the pages as desired.

8. Place remaining silhouetted photos on the pages as desired.

9. Using the die-cuts as "fillers," carefully slide them into place under and around silhouetted photos.

10. Apply adhesive to the back of each photo and die-cut. Adhere them onto the ground paper one at a time.

11. Using the markers, add journaling to the die-cuts, and ground paper.

areas, use a craft knife, as scissors may bend or tear the photo.

Design Tips:

Not all photos are right for this technique. If you have plenty of photos to use, give it a try. Use this technique sparingly throughout your album.

Choose just a few photos that depict the main event. This will give nice variety to the layout.

Photos with a blunt edge should be used toward the bottom of the page. Photos that can be cut all the way around can stand on their own.

To get into those hard-to-cut

me

I am **5** today!

Chantry

Taylor

Jordon

Erin

I got a: glow-in-the-dark sword, a nerf gun and my very own swimming pool!

How do I use stickers to embellish a page?

Jazz up any scrapbook page with inexpensive self-adhesive stickers. The variety is endless and the technique is quick and easy. These are also great for children to use when they are designing their own pages.

Hogle Zoo

Here's How:
1. Refer to Technique 7 on page 38. Round each corner of each photo.

2. Refer to Technique 2 on page 28. Adhere photos onto card stock. Cut the card stock ⅜" larger than the large photos all around and ¼" larger than the smaller photos all around.

3. Refer to Technique 1 on page 26. Arrange and adhere the photos onto the ground paper.

4. Carefully place stickers as desired to accent the page layout.

5. Add lettering to the page by carefully placing the letter stickers.

Troubleshooting:
When using stickers to add design to a page, try to keep the background very simple. Stickers tend to get "lost" on a heavily printed background; the page becomes very "busy," and the viewer's focus on the photos, the most important element, is diminished.

Remember, stickers are used to add to the story and perhaps a bit of color, not to become the reason you did the page in the first place. Be selective and use just a few stickers per page.

Design Tips:
Take your time placing the stickers. Some sticker brands allow you to remove the stickers and rearrange them before the adhesive becomes permanent, usually before 10–20 minutes.

If you are not certain where to place the sticker, do not peel it from the backing. Cut around the sticker, leaving the backing on, and lay it on the page to see how it looks. When you are satisfied, remove the backing and press the sticker onto the page. One time application is best with stickers, as removing and rearranging them causes the edges of the sticker to turn and sometimes bend.

What You Need to Get Started:

3 photos per page
Adhesive
Card stock: dark blue; burgundy; ginger speckled for ground paper; dark green
Corner rounder
Decorative-edged scissors: scallop; stamp; zigzag
Pencil
Scissors
Stickers: animals; letters
Transparent ruler

Hogle Zoo

Spring

1997

46

How do I use decorative papers that have borders?

Combine a piece of decorative paper that has a border with a photo or two, a small die-cut, and perhaps a few stickers, and you have an almost instant scrapbook page.

What You Need to Get Started:

1 class photo
1 portrait photo
Adhesive
Card stock: dark red
Decorative paper with border
Die-cuts: assorted
Pencil
Scissors
Template: oval
Transparent ruler

School Days

Here's How:

1. Using the transparent ruler, pencil, and scissors, measure, mark, and trim the class photo to fit within the border on the decorative paper.

2. Refer to Technique 6 on page 36. Crop the portrait photo as desired.

3. Refer to Technique 2 on page 28. Adhere the photo onto card stock. Cut the card stock ¼" larger than the photo all around.

4. Refer to Technique 1 on page 26. Arrange and adhere the photos and die-cuts onto the decorative paper.

Troubleshooting:

Avoid layering photos with a heavily printed paper as it becomes very busy and takes emphasis away from the border and more importantly, the photos. Use colored card stock to place behind photos. If your border is really busy, be selective about choosing die-cuts or stickers. Sometimes less is better.

47

13
technique

What You Need to Get Started:

3 photos per
   page
Acid-free paint
Adhesive
Adhesive dots:
   repositionable
   for stencils
Card stock: blue;
   brown; ivory
   for ground
   paper
Disposable
   palette
Makeup sponges
Paper towel
Pencil
Scissors
Stencil for
   memory page
Stickers: letters

Many stencils that were designed for decorative painting techniques easily cross over into the craft of scrapbooking. With just a bit of acid-free paint and a makeup sponge, you can add subtle colored images directly onto the ground paper.

Spring Lake

Note: Refer to photo on page 25 for facing page layout. I moved the stencil to place motifs in different areas.

Here's How:

1. Begin to create the border by centering the stencil along the bottom edge of the ground paper. Secure the stencil to the paper, using the re-positionable stencil dots.

2. Pour a small amount of paint onto disposable palette. Dip makeup sponge into paint. Dab sponge on paper towel, removing excess paint.

3. Apply paint from the edge of the stencil onto the ground paper, lightly dabbing to avoid bending the stencil. The paint will be darker around the fish and lighter as it reaches the edge of the paper. Allow the paint to dry.

4. Repeat Steps 1–3 for the top edge of the ground paper.

5. Clean the stencil and flip it over. Repeat Steps 1–3 for both sides of the ground paper.

6. Stencil-paint the frames, fish, fishing pole, water, and cattails onto the

ground paper, lightly dabbing to avoid bending the stencil, from the outside toward the center of the motif.

7. Refer to Technique 6 on page 36. Crop selected photos as desired.

8. Refer to Technique 1 on page 26. Arrange and adhere the photos onto the ground paper within the painted frames.

Troubleshooting:

Begin stenciling slowly. This is a technique which requires patience. Use a small amount of paint to avoid the paint seeping under the stencil.

How do I use creative lettering on a page?

What You Need to Get Started:

3 photos per page
Adhesive
Card stock: light blue speckled for ground paper; red; tan speckled; teal; white; yellow
Craft knife and cutting mat
Decorative-edged scissors: cloud; scallop; zigzag
Die-cuts: cloud; sun (2); umbrella
Lettering books
Light box
Markers: 0.5 mm black liner; 1.2 mm black liner; 0.5 mm baby blue liner; 1.2 mm baby blue liner; 1.2 mm red liner
Pencil
Self-adhesive die-cuts: glasses; pail; shovel; starfish (2)
Scissors
Templates: circle; oval; rectangle

A variety of lettering adds personality to any layout. Do not be afraid to experiment with different heights, widths, and colors of lettering on the same page. This technique is fun and very addicting.

Playa del Canto

Here's How:

1. Rip a piece of tan speckled card stock to create the "sand" and position it over the bottom portion of the ground paper.

2. Apply adhesive to the back of the torn paper. Adhere it onto the ground paper. Using scissors, trim tan speckled card stock flush with the ground paper.

3. Refer to Technique 6 on page 36. Crop selected photos as desired.

4. Refer to Technique 2 on page 28. Adhere photos onto card stock. Cut the card stock ¼" to ⅛" larger than each photo all around.

5. Using scissors, cut two pieces of white card stock for paper labels.

6. Place the selected lettering, right side up, on a light box with the white card stock on top, right side up. Using the pencil, lightly trace the lettering onto the card stock.

7. Using the markers, ink the lettering. Erase any pencil lines once the lettering is inked.

8. Adhere the lettered card stock onto colored card stock. Cut the colored card stock ¼" larger than each piece of lettered card stock all around.

9. Refer to Technique 1 on page 26. Arrange and adhere the photos, paper labels, and die-cuts onto the ground paper.

10. Using the markers, add journaling to the ground paper and die-cuts.

Trouble-shooting:
Ink the lettering before adhering the white card stock onto the colored card stock. If a mistake is made, the colored card stock is not wasted.

Design Tip:
To make certain the die-cuts appear as if they are down in the "sand," use

the craft knife to make a small slit in the tan card stock and slide the edge of the die-cut into the slit.

Mexico '97

digging for sand dollars

We buried Jake

How can I use rubber stamping to decorate a page?

Creating borders and backgrounds is simple with stamping. The most appealing aspect of working with rubber stamps is that the images can be used over and over without having to purchase the product every time.

What You Need to Get Started:

2 photos per page
Adhesive
Card stock: blue for ground paper; brown; tan
Colored pencils
Marker: 2.0 mm black calligraphy
Pencil
Permanent ink pad: black
Scissors
Stamp: sunflower
Transparent ruler

Jr. Performance

Here's How:

1. Refer to Technique 2 on page 28. Adhere photos onto tan card stock. Cut the card stock ⅛" larger than each photo all around.

2. Apply adhesive to the back of each piece of tan card stock. Adhere each piece onto brown card stock. Cut the brown card stock ⅛" larger than each piece of tan card stock all around.

3. Using transparent ruler, pencil, and scissors, measure, mark, and cut a 2¾" x 10½" strip of tan card stock.

4. Ink the sunflower stamp, using the black ink pad.

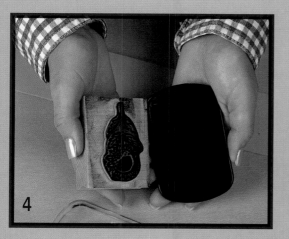

5. Print the image, by placing the stamp, rubber die side down, onto the card stock strip. Without rocking or twisting the stamp, give it a little pressure.

6. Lift the stamp straight up and off the card stock strip. Allow the ink to dry. Refer to photo on page 54.

7. Randomly print the image over the entire strip of card stock by repeating Steps 4–6.

6–7

11. Refer to Technique 1 on page 26. Arrange and adhere the photos onto the ground paper.

12. Using scissors, cut out the single stamped image, leaving ⅛" of card stock all around.

13. Apply adhesive to the back of the single stamped image. Adhere it onto the right side of the ground paper, overlapping the photo if desired.

14. Using the marker, add journaling to the page.

8. Print a single image onto a scrap piece of tan card stock. Allow the ink to dry.

9. Using the colored pencils, color the sunflowers as desired.

9

10. Apply adhesive to the back of the stamped card stock strip. Center and adhere it onto the left side of the ground paper.

Jr.
Performance
Group
'97–'98

54

How can I create 12" x 12" pages using 8½" x 11" stationery?

This is one of the funnest techniques to use. The variety of 8½" x 11" stationery is endless and converting these papers to 12" x 12" is so simple. Create your own borders, corner designs, and individual images from one piece of paper.

What You Need to Get Started:

1 photo per page
Adhesive
Card stock: olive green speckled; sage green; ivory speckled; light kraft for background paper; light peach for ground paper; rose; light yellow
Craft punch: heart
Decorative-edged scissors: deckle
Markers: 0.5 mm lavender liner; 1.2 mm lavender liner
Paper cutter
Pencil
Scissors
Stationery: Classic Pooh
Stickers: Classic Pooh
Transparent ruler

Big Hugs

Note: Refer to photos on page 25 for coordinating page layouts. I cut up stationery and placed motifs at the corners of the pages.

Here's How:

1. Using the transparent ruler, pencil, and paper cutter, measure, mark, and cut ¾" off the top and 1¾" off one side of light peach ground paper.

2. Apply adhesive to the back of the ground paper. Adhere it onto the light kraft background paper, ⅜" from the left side.

3. Apply adhesive to the back of the stationery. Adhere it onto the ground paper, ⅛" from the left side.

4. Refer to Technique 11 on page 45. Carefully place stickers at different angles down the right side of the background paper.

5. Refer to Technique 2 on page 28. Adhere the photo onto the sage green card stock. Cut the card stock ⅜" larger than the photo all around. Adhere the sage green card stock onto the ivory speckled card stock. Cut the ivory speckled card stock ⅛" larger than the sage green all around. Adhere the ivory speckled card stock onto the rose card stock. Cut the rose card stock ⅛" larger than the ivory speckled card all around.

6. Apply adhesive to the back of the rose card stock. Adhere it onto the stationery, 1" from the top and centered from side to side.

7. Cut the light yellow card stock to 3½" x 1" to create a paper label. Cut the olive green speckled card stock to 5" x 1¼".

8. Apply adhesive to the back of the yellow card stock. Adhere it onto the center of the olive green speckled card stock.

9. Refer to Technique 7 on page 38. Punch a heart from each side of olive green card stock on the paper label.

10. Using the markers, add journaling to the paper label.

11. Apply adhesive to the back of the paper label. Adhere it onto the stationery ¼" below the photo and centered from side to side on the stationery.

BIG HUGS

Breanna and Hannah '98

How do I use rub-ons to decorate a page?

Rub-ons are like using an oversized sticker—without the silhouette look that comes with a sticker. Rub-ons are great for layering and can be used on almost any surface.

What You Need to Get Started:

2 photos per
  page
Adhesive
Card stock: blue
  for ground
  paper; tan
  speckled for
  background
  paper
Corner rounder
Markers: 0.5 mm
  black liner;
  1.2 mm black
  liner
Paper cutter
Pencil
Rub-ons
Scissors
Transparent ruler

A Little Worn Out

Here's How:

1. Using the transparent ruler, pencil, and paper cutter, measure, mark, and cut ¾" from the top and one side of the ground paper.

2. Refer to Technique 7 on page 38. Round each corner of the ground paper.

3. Apply adhesive to the back of the ground paper. Adhere it onto the center of the background paper.

4. Cut out the selected rub-ons, leaving the paper backing attached to the rub-on.

5. Arrange the rub-ons and photos on the ground paper as desired.

6. Rub the design onto the ground paper and background paper.

7. Carefully remove the paper backing by lifting from one corner. Watch for the small black lines to make certain they have adhered onto the paper.

8. Apply adhesive to the back of each photo. Adhere them onto the ground paper one at a time.

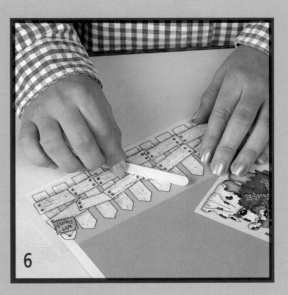

9. Using the markers, add journaling to the ground paper.

Trouble-shooting:
If you are uncertain where you are going to place the rub-on, cut around the motif, leaving the backing on, and lay it on the page to see how it looks.

When you are satisfied, remove the backing and press the rub-on onto the page.

One time application is best, as the back of the rub-on is very sticky and cannot be peeled up to be moved or it will tear apart.

Design Tip:
Do not be afraid to layer the designs—this is a great way to achieve dimension.

Feb. 1996

"a little worn out" DAVID 2½ yrs old

Wet Paint

How do I create puzzle pages?

Puzzle templates take all the guesswork out of cropping. This technique is easily accomplished and uses several pictures on one page. A puzzle page is a fun addition to any photo album.

Bathtime

Here's How:

1. Using the transparent ruler, pencil, and decorative-edged scissors, measure, mark, and cut 1½" off two sides of the ground paper.

2. Using scissors, cut two 1½" x 12" strips from the light kraft card stock. Using the decorative-edged scissors, trim one long edge from each strip.

3. Apply adhesive to the back of the ground paper along the scalloped edges. Position the scalloped light kraft card stock strips under the ground paper so about ¼" of light kraft is extending beyond the ground paper and adhere them together.

4. Apply adhesive to the back of the ground paper with the scalloped light kraft strips. Adhere it onto the center of the background paper.

5. Refer to Technique 6 on page 36. Crop selected photos as desired.

6. Using the template as a guide, arrange the photos on the page with even spacing.

7. Apply adhesive to the back of each photo. Adhere them onto the ground paper one at a time.

8. Using the marker, add journaling to the ground paper.

Troubleshooting:

Use a small piece of removable tape to hold photos in place while adhering each photo permanently. It is important to space each photo evenly to achieve the puzzle effect.

Design Tip:

Decide upon a theme and keep to that theme. Use large subjects for each opening to simplify the look of it.

What You Need to Get Started:

7 photos per page
Adhesive
Card stock: navy blue for ground paper; kraft for background paper; light kraft
Stencil: oval puzzle
Decorative-edged scissors: cloud
Marker: gold paint
Scissors

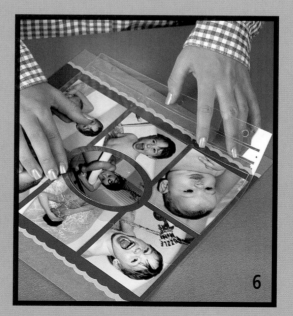

6

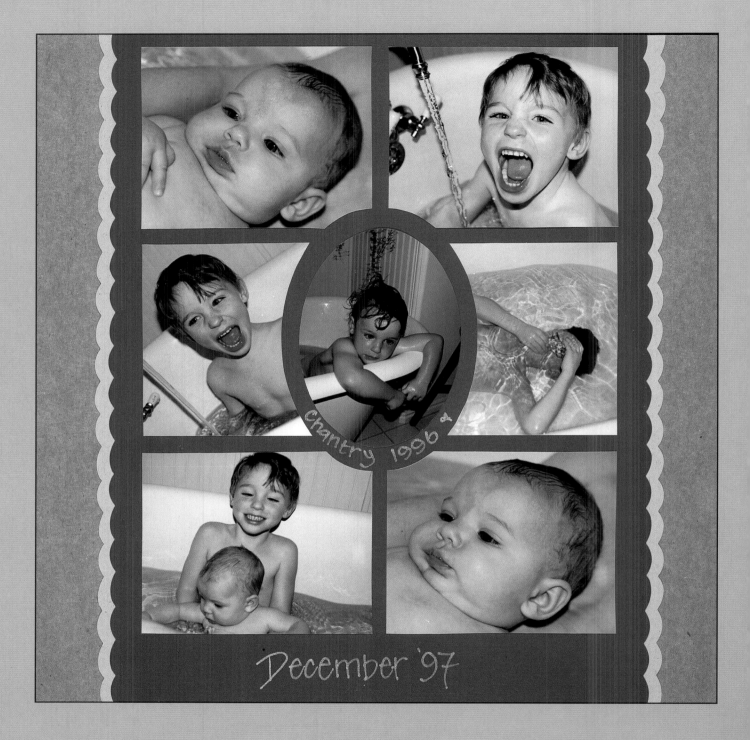

Chantry 1996

December '97

How do I use clip-art from pattern books?

This technique allows you to choose clip-art from books without using a computer. The images can be reduced or enlarged to fit the area you want to fill and may or may not be colored.

What You Need to Get Started:

4 photos per page
Acrylic paints and paintbrushes
Adhesive
Card stock: black for ground paper; blue; olive green; orange; rusty red; white; yellow for background paper
Corner rounder
Craft punch: star
Decorative-edged scissors: scallop; stamp; zigzag
Lettering books
Markers: 0.5 mm black liner; 1.2 mm black liner; 1.2 mm wheat liner
Paper cutter
Pattern book
Pencil
Scissors
Templates: circle; oval; rectangle
Transparent ruler
Watercolor paper: lightweight

Halloween '98

Note: Refer to photo on page 24 for facing page layout.

Here's How:

1. Using the transparent ruler, pencil, and paper cutter, measure, mark, and cut ⁵⁄₁₆" from the top and one side of the ground paper.

2. Refer to Technique 7 on page 38. Round each corner of the ground paper.

3. Punch a star in each corner of the ground paper.

4. Apply adhesive to the back of the ground paper. Adhere it onto the center of the background paper.

5. Refer to Technique 6 on page 36. Crop selected photos as desired.

6. Refer to Technique 2 on page 28. Adhere photos onto card stock. Cut the card stock ¼" to ⅛" larger than each photo all around or large enough to accommodate punching either on each corner or along one edge.

7. Punch stars from each corner of the selected card stock.

8. Select clip-art images from the pattern book. Using a photocopy machine, copy the images onto white card stock or watercolor paper, reducing or enlarging as desired.

8

9. Dilute acrylic paints with water to the consistency of a wash for a watercolor effect. Using the paintbrush, color the images as desired, beginning with a light wash and apply darker washes to create the shading. Allow paint to dry. Refer to photo on page 62.

9

Troubleshooting:

Choose designs that are easy to color. Make certain the designs do not overpower the page or compete with the photos.

Lay out your page and make certain the size of the clip-art works before adding color.

Color the image first before cutting it out. You can use colored pencils, markers, acrylic paints and paintbrushes, or watercolor paints and paintbrushes to color patterns. Seal these with an acrylic sealer.

Use scissors with a sharp point to cut around the colored image.

10. Using scissors, cut out images.

11. Refer to Technique 14 on page 50. Cut a piece of white card stock for paper label. Pencil and ink in the lettering.

12. Adhere the lettered card stock onto colored card stock. Cut the colored card stock ¼" larger than each piece of lettered card stock all around.

13. Refer to Technique 1 on page 26. Arrange and adhere the photos, clip-art images, punched stars, and paper label onto the ground paper.

How do I use computer clip-art?

In this technological age of computers, software made up of clip-art images is readily available and provides a quick and easy way to decorate a scrapbook page. Most clip-art programs contain both black line art and colored images.

What You Need to Get Started:

2 photos per page
Adhesive
Cardstock: sage green; orange; red for background paper
Computer clip-art
Decorative-edged scissors: zigzag
Paper: white
Paper cutter
Pencil
Scissors
Transparent ruler

Turkey Day

Here's How:

1. Refer to Technique 6 on page 36. Crop selected photos as desired.

2. Refer to Technique 2 on page 28. Adhere photos to card stock. Cut the card stock ¼" to ⅛" larger than the photos all around.

3. For reference, arrange the photos on a piece of white paper as desired.

4. Select clip-art images from the booklet provided with the computer clip-art. Arrange the images on a page in your document, positioning them to correspond with the layout of your photos, leaving ½" of white along the top and one side of the page.

5. Choose a coordinating font. Add journaling on your page by typing the information on the page within the document.

6. Print the page with the clip-art images and lettering. Using paper cutter, trim ½" from the top and one side of the printed page.

7. Apply adhesive to the back of the printed page. Adhere it onto the center of the red card stock.

8. Apply adhesive to the back of each photo. Adhere them onto the printed page one at a time.

Design Tip:

After choosing your photos for the page, measure the openings where the clip-art images will be placed. Size your image correctly before printing to save time that might otherwise be spent reducing or enlarging on a copy machine.

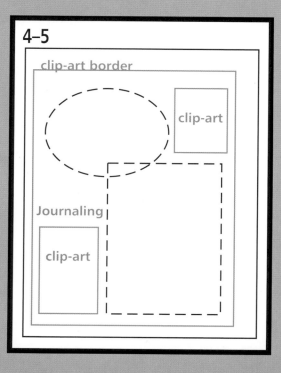

63

Turkey Day
November
1998

How do I make a pocket page to hold memorabilia?

The purpose of creating a scrapbook is to provide a place for keeping "scraps." Pocket pages are a wonderful way to keep special momentos close to the photos of the same event.

Rain Dance

Here's How:

1. Using transparent ruler, pencil, and scissors, measure, mark, and cut orange card stock to 5½" x 8½" for the pocket.

2. Punch holes along the top 8½" edge of the pocket, ⅜" apart.

3. Align the bottom edge of the pocket with the bottom edge of the ground paper. Using the paper punch, punch holes through both pieces of paper, ¾" apart all around.

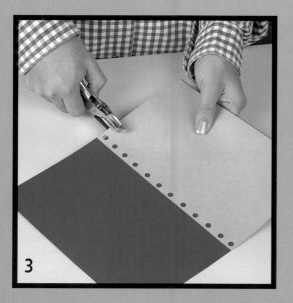

4. Tape one end of the jute to avoid fraying. Beginning at the top center hole of the pocket and leaving a 6" tail, weave the jute through the holes. Weave through both pieces of paper around the edges and finish weaving through the holes on the top of the pocket. Tie a bow where ends meet.

5. Using transparent ruler, pencil, and scissors, measure, mark, and cut a 4½" x 7½" piece of sage green card stock.

6. Refer to Technique 10 on page 43. Carefully cut around the photographic or copied image to be used for silhouetting.

What You Need to Get Started:

1 photo per page
Adhesive
Cardstock: sage green; orange; red for ground paper
Computer clip-art
Jute: 2-ply (1½ yards)
Memorabilia
Paper: white
Paper punch
Pencil
Scissors
Transparent ruler

7. Refer to Technique 20 on page 63. Prepare print, and cut out clip-art images and journaling.

8. Position the blunt edge of the silhouetted photo along the bottom of the sage green card stock. Arrange the clip-art images and journaling on the card stock as desired.

9. Apply adhesive to the back of each image. Adhere them onto the card stock one at a time.

10. Apply adhesive to the back of the sage green card stock. Adhere it onto the center of the pocket.

11. Place memorabilia into the pocket.

Troubleshooting:

Be aware that memorabilia-filled pocket pages may cause indentations on pages that are place next to them in a binder. Place these and pages with one-of-a-kind photos far apart.

During the month of November, we talked about Pilgrims and Indians. We made our own Indian costume and learned a lot of songs that I sang for my parents when I came home from school. My Mom's favorite song was T-U-R K-E-Y Turkey is my favorite and I'll tell you why... This is a picture of me showing Sophie my rain dance. She laughed and laughed as we danced in our backyard.

Design Tip:

There are kits available that you can use to create your own pocket pages in no time. The kits are themed and contain stickers, die-cut shapes, colored paper, patterned paper, adhesive strips, and step-by-step directions.

How do I use embossing templates to emboss paper?

Embossing is the nearly forgotten art of gently pressing a shape or motif into the paper's surface. While embossing is not a complex technique, it adds a wonderful texture and dimension to any page.

What You Need to Get Started:

1 large photo
Adhesive
Card stock: dark green; light green; dark lavender; light lavender; dark pink; light pink; pre-embossed white for ground paper
Embossing templates: flower; leaf
Scissors
Stylus
Tape

Little Angel

Here's How:

1. Refer to Technique 1 on page 26. Apply adhesive to the back of the photo. Adhere it at an angle onto the embossed ground paper.

2. Place the flower template on the front of the dark lavender card stock and lightly tape the stencil to the card stock.

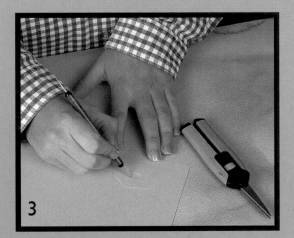

4. Using the scissors, carefully cut out the embossed flowers and leaves.

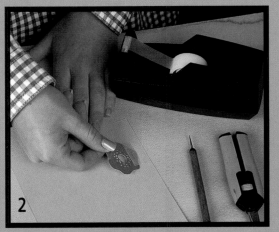

3. Turn the stencil over so the card stock is on top. Using the stylus, gently press the paper through the grooves of the template, creating a raised design. Repeat for a second flower.

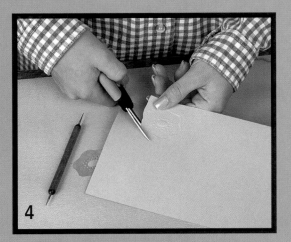

5. Repeat Steps 2–3 to emboss two

flowers onto light lavender card stock, two flowers onto dark pink card stock, and two flowers onto light pink card stock. Using the leaf template, emboss seven leaves onto dark green card stock and five leaves onto light green card stock.

6. Arrange and adhere the embossed flowers and leaves around each corner of the photo and onto the ground paper.

Troubleshooting:

Avoid scrubbing the stylus across larger areas of the design as this may leave grooves in the paper.

Because work is being done from the backside, the embossed design will be a reverse image of what is seen on the stencil front.

How do I use natural papers on a page?

What You Need to Get Started:

1 photo per page
Adhesive
Card stock: olive green; ivory; ivory for ground paper; pink speckled
Corner punch: fan
Corner rounder
Decorative paper: roses print for background paper
Decorative photo corners: black with leaf design
Decorative-edged scissors: deckle
Marker: 0.5 mm black liner
Natural paper
Paper cutter
Pencil
Stickers: green bow; pressed flowers; rose
Transparent ruler

Natural papers made with bits of flowers and leaves seem to lend new life to the photos. Most natural papers are hand-made and have a wonderful texture that stands out against the flatness of "run-of-the-mill" papers.

The Wedding

Here's How:

1. Using the transparent ruler, pencil, and paper cutter, measure, mark, and cut 1½" off the top and one side of the ground paper.

2. Refer to Technique 7 on page 38. Round each corner of the ground paper.

3. Apply adhesive to the back of the ground paper. Adhere it onto the center of the printed background paper.

4. Refer to Technique 2 on page 28. Adhere the photo onto the ivory card stock. Cut the card stock ¼" larger than the photo all around.

5. Refer to Technique 3 on page 30. Adhere the photo corners with the photo onto the olive green card stock. Cut the olive green card stock ⅜" larger than the ivory card stock all around.

6. Adhere the olive green card stock onto the natural paper. Cut the natural paper ⅜" larger than the olive green card stock all around.

7. Round each corner of the natural paper.

8. Adhere the natural paper onto the pink speckled card stock. Cut the pink speckled card stock ½" larger than the natural paper all around.

9. Punch each corner of the pink speckled card stock.

10. Apply adhesive to the back of the pink speckled card stock. Adhere it onto the ground paper, ½" from the top and centered from side to side.

11. Cut a piece of ivory card stock for a paper label. Punch each corner.

12. Adhere the ivory card stock onto the olive green card stock. Cut the olive green card stock ⅛" larger than the ivory card stock all around.

13. Using the marker, add journaling to the paper label.

14. Apply adhesive to the back of the olive green card stock. Adhere it onto the ground paper, ⅛" from the photo and centered from side to side.

15. Refer to Technique 11 on page 45. Carefully place the stickers on the ground paper and paper label as desired.

Troubleshooting:

Make certain you know where the natural stickers are going to be placed. These cannot be removed once they are placed onto the surface. They are extremely delicate, but well worth the extra care.

Design Tip:

If you want to give a photo an old-time look, create a small white border, using deckle decorative-edged scissors and some ivory card stock. This effect finishes a color copy made from an original.

How do I color-tint black-and-white photos?

Color-tinting black-and-white photos now is so easy, and spot pens have made it that much easier. This technique is almost like filling in the color in a coloring book.

Sunday Afternoon

Note: Carefully read all manufacturer's instructions for the photo tinting pen set. Refer also to photos on pages 2 and 24 for facing page layout.

Here's How:

1. To avoid scratching photos, soften pen tips by rubbing them vigorously on a discarded photo for 20 seconds.

2. Using a sponge, moisten the area to be colored with water and solution provided in the photo tinting set. Make two or three swipes with the sponge from top to bottom or from side to side so the photo is slightly tacky, but not wet.

3. Lightly touch the pen tip to the black-and-white photo. Fill in the area, using circular motions and gradually building color.

What You Need to Get Started:

2 photos per page
Adhesive
Card stock: blue speckled; brown speckled ; olive green speckled; olive green speckled for background paper; sage green speckled; ivory; light kraft speckled for ground paper; lavender; plum; yellow
Decorative border: light brown with vine design
Decorative corner punch: fan
Decorative photo corners: light brown with vine design
Decorative-edged scissors: deckle
Marker: 0.5 mm black liner
Natural paper
Paper cutter
Pencil
Pressed flowers
Scissors
Self-adhesive laminate
Spot pens: photo tinting set
Templates: circle; oval; rectangle; square
Transparent ruler

Note: If streaking occurs, either the photo has become too dry and needs to be moistened again or you are using too dark a color on a light area.

4. Using a cotton swab, blot excess dye from the photo.

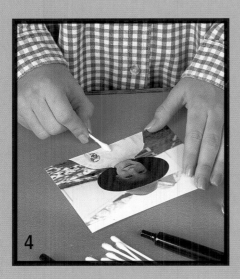

5. Using the transparent ruler, pencil, and paper cutter, measure, mark, and cut 1" off the top and one side of the ground paper.

6. Refer to Technique 7 on page 38. Punch each corner of the ground paper.

7. Apply adhesive to the back of the ground paper. Adhere it onto the center of the back-ground paper.

8. Refer to Technique 6 on page 36. Crop selected photos as desired.

9. For each photo, refer to Technique 2 on page 28. Adhere photos onto coordin-ating pieces of card stock and natural paper. Cut the card stock and natural paper ⅝", ⅜", and ¼" larger than the photo all around.

10. Refer to Technique 3 on page 30. For selected photos, adhere photos with photo corners onto the center of the smallest piece of natural paper or card stock.

11. For remaining photos, adhere the photo onto the center of the smallest piece of natural paper or card stock. Repeat the process for the remaining pieces of natural paper or card stock for the desired number of paper layers.

12. Measure, mark, and cut ivory card stock to 2⅜" x 2" for a paper label. Trim off corners.

13. Adhere the ivory card stock onto the lavender card stock. Cut the lavender card stock ⅜" larger than the ivory card stock all around. Punch each corner of the lavender card stock.

14. Using the marker, add journaling to the paper label.

15. Measure, mark, and cut four 1¾" squares, one 2" circle, one 2⅝" oval, and one 2½" x 5" rectangle from ivory card stock.

16. Adhere each piece of ivory card stock onto a coordinating piece of card stock. Cut coordinating pieces of card stock ⅛" larger than each piece of ivory card stock all around.

17. Position pressed flowers on the ivory card stock as desired. Apply adhesive to the back of each flower. Adhere them onto the card stock. Following manufacturer's instructions, apply self-adhesive laminate over the card stock to enclose the pressed flowers.

18. Apply adhesive to the back of the decorative border. Adhere it onto the ground paper ⅞" from the left or bottom edge.

19. Refer to Technique 1 on page 26. Arrange and adhere photos, paper label, and pressed flower cards onto the ground sheet as desired.

Troubleshooting:

Save all the photos you may have otherwise discarded so you can practice the tinting technique on them. This is not only for selecting color place-ment but also for experimenting with the moisture needed on the photo to avoid streaking. It is better to practice on a few disposable photos than on a photo that may be difficult to replace.

Design Tip:

Sometimes less color is better. Some photos may need only one or two colors to be the most dramatic.

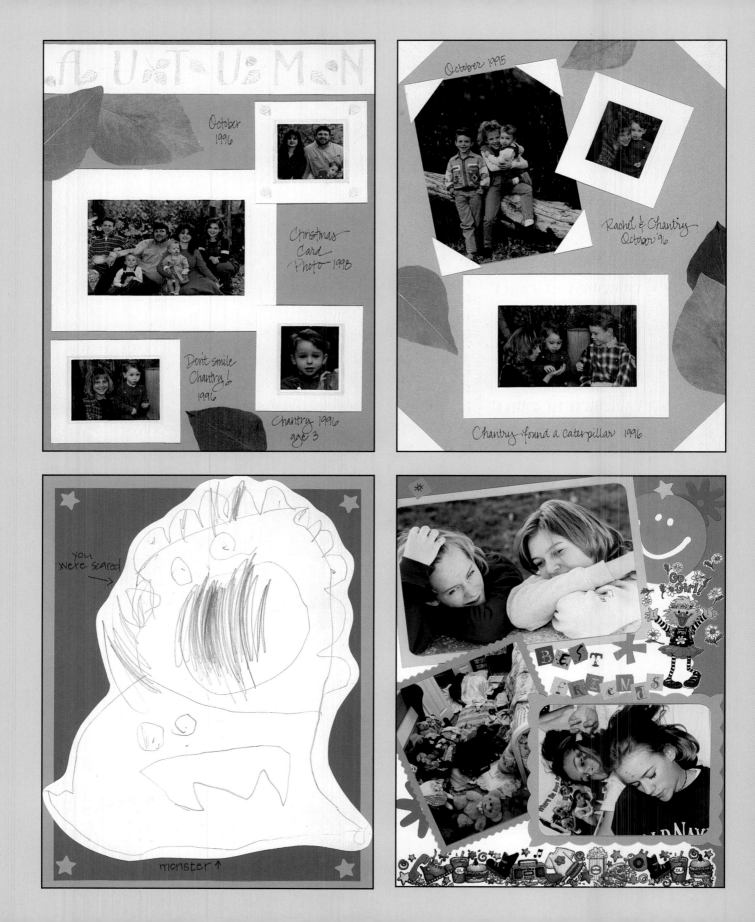

A U T U M N

October 1996

Christmas Card Photo 1998

Don't smile Chantry! 1996

Chantry 1996 age 3

October 1995

Rachel & Chantry October '96

Chantry found a caterpillar 1996

You were scared →

monster ↑

BEST FRIENDS

Go Girl!

Section 3: *projects beyond the basics*

How do I create a "teen" page?

These types of pages are great because "anything goes." The more the better. This technique fits the personality of the theme and is exciting to look at.

What You Need to Get Started:

3 photos per page
Adhesive
Card stock: lime green; hot pink; teal; white for ground paper; bright yellow
Decorative-edged scissors: cloud; scallop; zigzag
Die-cuts: assorted
Lettering book
Markers: 1.2 mm black liner; 1.2 mm green liner
Paper label
Pencil
Scissors
Stickers
Templates: circle; rectangle; square

Life as a Teen

Note: Refer to photo on page 74 for facing page layout.

Here's How:

1. Using the transparent ruler, pencil, and zigzag decorative-edged scissors, measure, mark, and cut ¾" from the top and one side of the ground paper.

2. Apply adhesive to the back of ground paper. Adhere it onto background paper, lining up the two uncut edges and leaving a colored border on the left and top edges. If you have a facing page, repeat with another piece of ground paper and background paper, leaving a colored border on the right and top edges.

3. Refer to Technique 6 on page 36. Crop selected photos as desired.

4. Refer to Technique 2 on page 28. Adhere photos onto card stock. Cut the card stock ¼" to ⅛" larger than each photo all around.

5. Refer to Technique 14

on page 50. Pencil and ink in the lettering on the paper label.

6. Refer to Technique 1 on page 26. Arrange and adhere photos, paper label, and die-cuts onto the ground paper.

7. Refer to Technique 11 on page 45. Carefully place the stickers on the ground paper as desired.

How can I display dimensional items on a page?

Incorporate purchased memorabilia pockets into your page design to display items that have real or sentimental value. These durable pockets keep small items safe and sound.

5 photos per page
Adhesive
Card stock: navy blue; navy blue for background paper; brown; ivory; light kraft for ground paper; dark tan; light tan
Color copies of green leaves
Decorative-edged scissors: deckle; zigzag
Jute: 2-ply (1½ yards per page)
Markers: 0.5 mm black liner; 5.0 mm brown calligraphy
Memorabilia
Memorabilia pockets: self-adhesive
Natural paper
Paper cutter
Paper punch
Scissors
Tape
Templates: circle; oval; rectangle; square

Kids in Our Neighborhood

Note: Before creating the scrapbook page, gather some autumn leaves and place them between two layers of paper toweling. Stack heavy books on top of the toweling. Allow the leaves to dry for approximately two weeks. Take the leaves to a professional copy shop and have them color copied.

If leaves are out of season, they can be purchased already pressed. They are expensive so take good care of them and they can be used over and over.

Refer to photo on page 75 for facing page layout.

Here's How:
1. Using the transparent ruler, pencil, and paper cutter, measure, mark, and cut ½" off the top and one side of the ground paper.

2. Using the paper punch, punch holes ½" apart all around the edges of the ground paper.

3. Tape one end of the jute to avoid fraying. Beginning at the top right hole of the ground paper, weave the jute through the holes all around.

4. Apply adhesive to the back of the ground paper. Adhere it onto the center of the background paper.

5. Position the natural paper at an angle on the ground paper. Using the scissors, trim the corners of the natural paper flush with the inside edge of the punched holes.

6. Refer to Technique 6 on page 36. Crop selected photos as desired.

7. Refer to Technique 2 on page 28. Adhere photos onto card stock. Cut the card stock ¼" to ⅛" larger than each photo all around. If desired, adhere this piece of card stock onto a second piece of card stock. Cut the second piece of card stock ¼" to ⅛" larger than the first piece of card stock all around.

8. To create photo labels and layered paper for memorabilia pockets, cut two pieces of ivory card stock. Adhere each piece of ivory card stock onto a coordinating piece of card stock. Cut the coordinating piece of card stock ¼" larger than the ivory card stock all around.

9. Remove the paper backing from the adhesive on the back of the memorabilia pocket. Adhere the pocket onto

the center of the ivory card stock on the selected layered piece.

10. Refer to Technique 14 on page 50. Using the markers, add lettering and journaling to the paper labels.

11. Using scissors, cut out the color copied leaves, making edges wavy for a realistic look.

12. Refer to Technique 1 on page 26. Arrange and adhere the photos, memorabilia pockets, photo labels, and leaves onto the ground paper.

13. Fill the pockets with memorabilia.

How can I display my child's artwork on a scrapbook page?

Photos are not the only things that are displayed in a scrapbook. It is a great place to put artwork. It tells such a wonderful story about a child, and they are so proud to see it displayed in book form.

A Monster Under Your Blanket

Here's How:

1. Using the transparent ruler, pencil, and paper cutter, measure, mark, and cut ¾" off the top and one side of the ground paper.

2. Refer to Technique 7 on page 38. Punch a star in each corner of the ground paper.

3. Apply adhesive to the back of the ground paper and adhere it to the center of the background paper.

4. Refer to Technique 6 on page 36. Crop selected photos as desired.

5. Refer to Technique 2 on page 28. Adhere photos onto card stock. Cut the card stock ¼" to ⅛" larger than each photo all around.

6. Using the marker, add journaling to the paper label.

7. Refer to Technique 1 on page 26. Arrange and adhere the child's artwork, paper label, and photos onto the ground paper.

8. Using the marker, add any additional children's drawings and journaling to the ground paper.

Design Tip:

Instead of using stickers to decorate the pages, have your child draw some borders or small items to decorate the pages. It will make it much more personable.

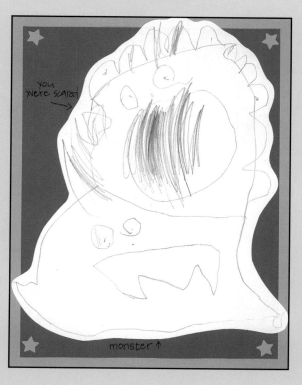

What You Need to Get Started:

2 photos per page
Adhesive
Card stock: green; green for ground paper; orange for background paper; red for ground paper; yellow; yellow for background paper
Child's artwork
Craft punch: star
Decorative-edged scissors: scallop; zigzag
Paper cutter
Paper label
Pencil
Marker: 0.5 mm black liner
Scissors
Templates: circle; rectangle

"Mom this is when a monster was under your blanket"

Chantry age 4

March 24, 1998

ghost team monster

ghost monster

Suzy's Zoo ®

How should I use bright colors?

Summer time usually means bright and fun colors. Keep the ground paper simple and the photos will pop off the page.

Tessa & Rylee

Here's How:
1. Using the cloud decorative-edged scissors, trim the ground paper ¼" all around.

2. Apply adhesive to the back of the ground paper. Adhere it onto the center of the background paper.

3. Refer to Technique 6 on page 36. Crop selected photos as desired.

4. Refer to Technique 2 on page 28. Adhere photos onto card stock. Cut the card stock ¼" to ⅛" larger than each photo all around.

5. Refer to Technique 1 on page 26. Arrange and adhere the photos and die-cuts onto the ground paper.

6. Using the markers, add journaling to cloud die-cut.

What You Need to Get Started:

3 photos per page
Adhesive
Card stock: neon green; neon pink; teal for ground paper; white for background paper; bright yellow
Decorative-edged scissors: cloud; scallop; zigzag
Die-cuts: cloud; flower; palm tree; star; sun; swirl
Markers: 0.5 mm black liner; 1.2 mm black liner
Pencil
Templates: oval; rectangle
Scissors

Tessa & Rylee
1998

5 project

How do I use a full kit to design several pages?

This is a simple way of assembling many pages at once without having to buy many components. Depending on the company that compiled it, a kit contains a variety of materials from the background paper and framed corners to separate frames and labels, to decorative pieces.

What You Need to Get Started:

4 photos per page
Adhesive
Card stock: olive green speckled; plum; tan speckled
Color copies of leaves
Colored pencils
Marker: 0.5 mm black liner
Pencil
Scissors
Scrapbook kit
Tape

Fall Colors

Note: Refer also to photos on pages 74 and 75 for coordinating page layouts.

Here's How:

1. Divide the kit into separate pages. Carefully punch out the die-cut borders and images.

2. Coordinate the premade photo mattes with the photos. Using scissors, trim selected photos as necessary.

3. Refer to Technique 4 on page 32. Place premade photo mattes face down on the work surface. Center each photo face down on the matte. Place tape on the sides of each photo matte and adhere each photo.

4. Using the colored pencils, lightly color the embossed areas to tint the images.

5. Refer to Project 2 on page 77. Using scissors, cut out the color copied leaves.

6. Refer to Technique 1 on page 26.

Arrange and adhere the matted photos and leaves onto ground paper.

7. Using the marker, add journaling to the pages.

Design Tips:

I loved using this embossed kit. It came with eight pages—two completely ready and four that I could create myself, using the frames and corners that were provided.

I chose the fall packet because I have many pictures from past years' Christmas card photos. I have a pile of photographer's proofs that fit many of the smaller frames. Proofs are a great way to fill several pages because not everyone looks good in every photo. Cropping out someone who may have had their eyes closed or who was looking in another direction places the focus on the person who looks great. This makes the most of your photos.

You do not have to stay with the exact kit unless it fits everything you like. Do not be afraid to replace the ground sheet with a piece of colored card stock.

When using colored pencils to tint the embossed images, do not use a sharp point. Sharp points create lines that are not very attractive. Dull the pencil point by first coloring several strokes on a piece of scratch paper, creating a flat edge. A dull point makes a nice even color on the embossed image. You are high-lighting the embossed image and therefore should color only the top surface of the image and avoid coloring down into the engraved areas or around the sides. Do not press hard or you may dent the embossed image. Several light applications will achieve a darker color.

Watercolors or water-based, blendable pens will also work for tinting the em-bossed images.

Some kits only come in 8½" x 11". If you need some-thing to fit a 12" x 12" album format, you can off-set the 8½" x 11" framed sheet to one side of the 12" x 12" ground sheet.

Adhere a piece of card stock to the back of any embossed frame complete with photos that is the size of a page. The cardstock will protect the back side of the photos.

MEMORIES

Christmas Card Photo October 1996

Rachel 1996

Chantry 1996

Sophie did not want to smile! 1998

How can I use stationery cut-outs to decorate a page?

What You Need to Get Started:

5 photos per page
Adhesive
Card stock: blue; green; kraft for ground paper; red; white; yellow
Craft knife and cutting mat
Decorative-edged scissors: scallop; stamp; zigzag
Markers: 0.5 mm black liner; 1.2 mm black liner
Scissors
Stationery: patterned 8½" x 11"
Templates: circle; oval; rectangle
Transparent ruler

Stationery is so versatile. Cut out individual images from one sheet of stationery to decorate one scrapbook page. You can use a full sheet of stationery on facing scrapbook page to complement the first with journaling or additional photos.

Boys & Bugs

Here's How:

1. Using the craft knife or scissors, carefully cut out the images from the patterned stationery.

2. Refer to Technique 6 on page 36. Crop selected photos as desired.

3. Refer to Technique 2 on page 28. Adhere photos to card stock. Cut the card stock ¼" to ⅛" larger than each photo all around.

4. Arrange the cut-out images on the page to create a border. Arrange the photos on the page as desired. Fill in any large gaps with cut-out images.

5. Adhere the cut-out images and photos onto the ground paper one at a time.

6. Using the markers, add journaling to the ground paper.

How do I create theme pages?

Because there are so many products available, a theme page is easy to assemble. Add a few momentos and some stickers and the page quickly comes together.

Mickey & Friends

Here's How:

1. Using the transparent ruler, pencil, and paper cutter, measure, mark, and cut 1" off the top and 2" off one side of the ground paper.

2. Apply adhesive to the back of the ground paper. Adhere it onto the background paper, ½" from the left side and centered top to bottom.

3. Refer to Technique 6 on page 36. Crop the selected photos as desired.

4. Refer to Technique 2 on page 28. Adhere the photos onto the blue, green, and red card stock. Cut the card stock ¼" larger than each photo all around.

5. Refer to Technique 1 on page 26. Arrange and adhere the memorabilia, photos, and punch-outs onto the ground paper

6. Using the markers, add journaling to the ground paper.

7. Refer to Technique 11 on page 45. Carefully place the stickers on the ground paper as desired.

What You Need to Get Started:

3 photos per page
Adhesive
Card stock: blue; green; red; yellow plaid for ground paper
Decorative paper: theme print for background paper
Marker: 0.5 mm black liner
Memorabilia
Paper cutter
Punch-outs: theme motifs
Scissors
Stickers: numbers
Templates: circle; oval; rectangle
Transparent ruler

How can I get the most out of my stationery?

Assemble two or more layouts from one page of stationery by cutting out each image, creating any size of surface area. You will stretch your supplies and your money.

What You Need to Get Started:

2 photos per page
Adhesive
Card stock:
  blue; light
  blue; green;
  light green;
  ivory; ivory for
  ground paper;
  light kraft;
  light kraft for
  background
  paper; pink;
  rose; white;
  light yellow
Decorative-
  edged scissors:
  deckle
Marker: 0.5 mm
  brown liner
Paper cutter
Pencil
Scissors
Stationery with
  multiple motifs

Peter Ty

Here's How:
1. Using the transparent ruler, pencil, and paper cutter, measure, mark, and cut 1½" off the top and one side of the ground paper.

2. Apply adhesive to the back of the ground paper. Adhere it onto the center of the background paper.

3. Using scissors, cut out motifs from the stationery, leaving a ⅛" silhouette all around each image.

4. Apply adhesive to the back of each silhouetted image. Adhere them onto light shades of coordinating card stock and cut each piece of card stock ⅛" larger than the image on four sides.

5. Apply adhesive to the back of each piece of card stock. Adhere them onto darker shades of coordinating card stock, allowing enough space around each for creating a paper "frame."

Using scissors, cut each piece of card stock ⅛" larger than the first all around.

6. Refer to Technique 2 on page 28. Adhere each photo onto ivory card stock. Cut card stock ⅛" larger than the combined photos all around.

7. Apply adhesive to the back of each photo. Adhere them side by side, ¼" apart, onto light blue card stock, allowing enough space all around for creating a paper "frame." Using scissors, cut card stock ¼" larger than the photos all around.

8. Measure, mark, and cut a 5" x 1⅛" piece of ivory card stock to create a paper label. Adhere the ivory card stock onto brown card stock. Cut the brown card stock ⅛" larger than the ivory card stock all around.

9. Using the brown marker, add journaling to the ivory card stock.

10. Apply adhesive to the back of two remaining silhouetted images. Adhere them onto the paper label.

11. Arrange and adhere the images, photos, and the paper label onto the ground paper.

Peter Ty
6 months 1962

9 project

What You Need to Get Started:

3 photos per
   page
Adhesive
Card stock: ivory
Craft knife and
   cutting mat
Decorative paper:
   print with
   frames
Marker: 0.5 mm
   black liner
Scissors
Tape

How do I use paper with printed frames?

The page design is already created for you. Simply insert your favorite photos. This process makes completing several pages in one sitting quick and worry-free.

Tori Anne

Here's How:

1. Using the craft knife and cutting mat, cut out openings within printed frames on the decorative paper.

2. Refer to Technique 4 on page 32. Treat this piece of paper as a premade photo matte. Place paper face down on the work surface. Center each photo face down on the openings. Tape the sides of each photo to the back of the paper.

3. Apply adhesive to the back of the paper complete with photos. Adhere it to a piece of card stock that is the same size as the decorative paper. The cardstock will protect the back side of the photos.

4. Using the marker, add journaling to the page.

How do I use different patterned papers together?

Layering different patterned papers is a great way to make one photo on a page stand out. Do not be afraid to use several papers on one page.

What You Need to Get Started:

1 photo per page
Adhesive
Card stock: dark blue; light blue speckled
Decorative-edged scissors: zigzag
Marker: 1.2 mm black liner
Paper: blue plaid for background paper; tan striped; tan striped for ground paper
Paper cutter
Pencil
Scissors
Template: rectangle
Transparent ruler

August 1994

Here's How:

1. Using the pencil, transparent ruler, and paper cutter, measure, mark, and cut 2" off the top and one side of the ground paper.

2. Apply adhesive to the back of the ground paper. Adhere it onto the center of the background paper.

3. Refer to Technique 6 on page 36. Crop the photo as desired.

4. Refer to Technique 2 on page 28. Adhere the photo onto the light blue speckled card stock. Cut the light blue card stock ¼" larger than the photo all around.

5. Adhere the light blue speckled card stock onto the dark blue card stock. Cut the dark blue card stock ¼" larger than the light blue speckled card stock all around.

6. Adhere the dark blue card stock onto the ground paper, ⅜" from the top and centered from side to side.

7. To make a paper label, cut a 3½" x 1" piece of tan striped paper. Adhere the tan striped paper onto dark blue card stock. Cut the dark blue card stock ⅛" larger than the tan striped paper all around.

8. Adhere the dark blue card stock onto light blue speckled card stock. Cut the light blue speckled card stock ⅛" larger than the dark blue card stock all around.

9. Using the marker, add journaling to the paper label.

10. Adhere the light blue speckled card stock onto the ground paper, ¼" from the photo and centered from side to side.

Are there premade pages I can use?

Premade keepsake kits are a great way to record events that share a common theme and are accompanied by a lot of photos, such as a wedding or birth of a baby.

What You Need to Get Started:

2–4 photos per page
Adhesive
Card stock: lavender; peach; pink; yellow
Keepsake kit: text; borders and backgrounds
Markers: 0.5 mm black liner; 0.5 mm lavender liner; 1.2 mm lavender liner
Memorabilia
Pencil
Scissors
Transparent ruler

Keepsake Kits

Note: The kits are made up of two parts. The first includes a variety of borders with text for recording information, such as the mother's thoughts during pregnancy, the birth statistics, the family tree, the birth certificate, the baby's prints, and a year of journaling month to month events. The second kit includes frames, borders, backgrounds, and stickers.

Kits are available in both the 12" x 12" and 8½" x 11" formats.

Here's How:
1. Refer to Technique 6 on page 36. Crop selected photos as desired.

2. Refer to Technique 2 on page 28. Adhere photos onto card stock. Cut the card stock ¼" to ⅛" larger than each photo all around.

3. Refer to Technique 1 on page 26. Arrange and adhere photos and memorabilia onto the ground paper.

4. Refer to Technique 11 on page 45. Carefully place the stickers on the ground paper as desired.

5. Using markers, add journaling to the page.

Sophie
- 20 minutes old
- 3 hours
- 24 hours

The Big Day

I was due to arrive on September 9th '97

Labor began on September 9th at

1 p.m. After 5½ hours, I was born at 5:45 p.m.

on Sept. 9th The birth took place at

American Fork Birthing Center

with Dr. Lamoreaux making the delivery.

Rachel was the first person to hold me and the

first to hear the happy news were Grandpa & Grandma Sommer, Grandpa & Grandma Carter, Kathy, Jo, Irene, Tyrel, Chantry, Stewarts, Fullers & Ember

I look like my brother, Chantry

The first impressions of me were she's finally here and she looked like she was three months old!! She was so bruised because she was so large & difficult to deliver. Almost ten pounds!

My name was chosen by Mom & Rachel

because mom loved the name & was discovered it was also a relative's name. Lucille because Rachel & I love Lucille Ball.

A Little Girl to Fill Your Home with Love

Memorable Moments

My first		I first	
bath	2 wks	rolled tummy to back	6 mo.
tooth	2/25/98	slept through the night	13 mo.
smile	10/6/97	held a bottle	1 yr.
coos	11/2/97	held a toy	12/1/97
face recognition	1 mo.	sat alone	1/30/98
laugh	12/4/97	crawled	4/26/98
baby food	1 yr.	stood with assistance	6 mo.
table food	11 mo.	stood alone	11 mo.
word		took my first step	1 yr.
word was		drank from a cup	10 mo.
kisses	6/20/98	waved good-bye	1 yr.
		clapped my hands	4/1/98
		discovered my feet	1/31/98
		saw my hand	11/1/97

12
project

How do I create calendar pages?

What You Need to Get Started:

4 photos per page
12-month calendar: blank
Adhesive
Card stock: blue; green; red; teal; yellow
Craft punch: star
Decorative-edged scissors: cloud; scallop; zigzag
Markers: 0.5 mm black liner
Pencil
Scissors
Stickers: assorted
Templates: oval; rectangle

Making a scrapbook from a calendar is a wonderful way to keep a record of the special events that happen every day. Later, because you took the time to write it down on your calendar, you will be able to remember when and what happened and make certain that it is also recorded in your journal or scrapbook. Combined with favorite photos, it becomes a mini scrapbook to look at from year to year.

School Memories

Here's How to Create September:
1. Refer to Technique 6 on page 36. Crop selected photos as desired.

2. Refer to Technique 2 on page 28. Adhere photos onto coordinating card stock. Using scissors, cut the card stock ¼" larger than the photo on the sides and bottom and ⅞" larger on the top. Cut the card stock ⅜" larger than the oval photo on four sides, creating a rectangle. Using the decorative-edged scissors, cut the card stock ¼" larger than two remaining rectangle photos all around.

3. Refer to Technique 7 on page 38. Punch a star in each corner of the oval photo's card stock frame. Punch stars along the wide edge of the rectangle photo's card stock frame.

4. Refer to Technique 1 on page 26. Arrange and adhere photos onto the blank page.

5. Refer to Technique 11 on page 45. Carefully place the stickers onto the photo page as desired. Carefully place stickers onto the calendar page that coordinate with the recorded events.

6. Using the marker, add journaling to the photo page.

Here's How to Create May:
1. Refer to Technique 6 on page 36. Crop selected photos as desired.

2. Refer to Technique 2 on page 28. Adhere photos onto coordinating card stock. Cut the card stock ¼" larger than the photos all around.

3. Refer to Technique 1 on page 26. Arrange and adhere photos onto the blank page.

4. Refer to Technique 11 on page 45. Carefully place the stickers onto the photo page as desired. Carefully place stickers onto the calendar page that coordinate with the recorded events.

5. Using the marker, add journaling to the photo page.

Design Tip:
Use the calendar to record the small day-to-day events, such as your child's first word, the day you collected flowers, dance recitals, etc.

HAPPY BIRTHDAY

First day of school

to me!!!!

AaBbCc

Chantry's
Pre-school Graduation
May 27th

Happy Birthday!

Sophies first time on the grass!

Rachel and Chantry

School Daze
September

Sunday	Monday	Tuesday	Wednesday	Thursday	Friday	Saturday
		First Day of School 1	2	Chantry chose his school box & pencils 3	4	5
6	ordered Seasame Street Cake 7	First Day of Kindergarten Chantry was ready @ 7a.m. 8	Sophie's 1st Birthday 9	10	Chantry brings home his first homework 11	12
Chantry's First Prayer 13	14	15	16	Chantry's First Dentist Appt. 17	Sophie takes her first step 18	19
Primary Program 20	21	Sophies First Word "Dad" 22	23	Tyrel's Fall Program 24	25	26
27	Tyrel Student of the week 28	29	Rachel's Dance Recital 30			

Good Job!

© Pebbles in my Pocket ®

May

Sunday	Monday	Tuesday	Wednesday	Thursday	Friday	Saturday
					1	Sophie climbs up the stairs 2
3	4	5	6	7	Sophies first time on the grass 8	Tyrel picks flowers for me. 9
Mother's Day Program 10	11	12	13	Chantry picks out his favorite flower to plant 14	15	Planted Flowers 16
17	Rachel's Birthday Family Party 7pm. 18	Chantry's Birthday 19	20	21	22	23
24 / 31	25	Chantrys Pre-school Program 26	27	28	Last Day of school 29	Went to the park 30

© Pebbles in my Pocket ®

Happy Birthday

Life's simple pleasures...
Henry's Fork
1997

Elli & Grady

Hotel Burley
STRICTLY MODERN   E. A. GRANT
BURLEY, IDAHO

Section 4: *gallery*

Pauline Locke (pictured left when she was a young girl) was born "a long time ago" in London, England. She was educated at Camden High School and then completed a course in design at the London College of Printing.

You Can Run BUT YOU Can't HidE

designed by Pauline Locke

Founder's Day Picnic

foot race

designed by Pauline Locke

designed by Pauline Locke

She has worked for many years as an illustrator for clients such as Hendersons Publishing, Anness Books, And So to Bed, Polytint Cards, and the BBC.

Pauline has two daughters, Kate and Rebecca, and one grandson, Milan. She currently resides in Ogden, Utah, with her husband, Andy.

Today, in art class, we went outside to study the effects of light.
We talked about the impressionists and our teacher, Gerry, had us draw a few sketches of each other.

designed by Pauline Locke

Shirley Pilkington
(pictured above left with her granddaughter, Rose) attended Weber State University with an emphasis in Literature and English. Her poetry has been published on several occasions.

After only six months of scrapbooking, Shirley was hooked and opened up her own store, Daisy Dots & Doodles. She teaches scrapbooking classes several times a week and also designs scrapbook kits and papers. Shirley's own pages are full of texture and dimension and have been published in several scrapbook magazines.

designed by Shirley Pilkington

Shirley lives in a beautiful rural town where she and her husband, Gary, are active in their church and community. She is the mother of three children and the grand-mother of six, which gives her a multitude of photo opportunities for her scrapbook pages.

designed by Shirley Pilkington

designed by Becky Hunsaker

Becky Hunsaker started scrapbooking in 1995 after the loss of an infant son. She wanted to do a special book in his memory and also continue the memories with her two other sons. She was instantly addicted and since that time has completed many books, including a 50th anniversary book for her parents, a book for her husband, a grandpa book, a family photo book, and, of course, she continues to work on her children's books. She hopes one day to do her own.

Becky works at Memories by Design, where she teaches a Scrapbook Basics class. She likes to create fun, simple pages that do not detract from the photos. She also loves to add simple verses or journal entries to her pages.

Her other hobbies include sewing, reading, bowling, and spending time with her family. She has experienced many emotions through scrapbooking—from the healing of a broken heart to the excitement of learning more about her heritage, to the thrill of hearing the giggles of her boys as they look at their books.

No Gurlz Allowed!

Life's simple pleasures...
Henry's Fork
1997

designed by Becky Hunsaker

Brianna Johnson started scrapbooking four years ago when her first child was born. It was such a joy for her to capture moments of life that she never wanted to forget. Now, instead of keeping a journal, she makes scrapbooks. She has one book for each year of each of her children's lives.

Recently, Brianna started her own professional photography business, which she finds both challenging and rewarding. She is very active and one of her favorite sports is rock climbing.

Brianna, her husband, Ryan, and their children Cloe (4), and Gavin (1) all enjoy looking back at those memories which they can remember again and again because they are recorded in her scrapbooks.

Nancy Freebairn started scrapbooking as a teenager with a love for both photography and art. Her interests led her to a career in photo retouching and restoration.

In 1995 Nancy discovered the "new" style of scrapbooking and found that the craft incorporated all the aspects of the art that she enjoyed.

Her enjoyment of the craft continues today and she tries to scrapbook whenever she can. She says her biggest challenge is just keeping up.

Nancy and her husband, Eric, are the parents of four great kids, Chase (11), Amanda (8), Alyssa (3), and Tyler (3 mos.).

When she is not scrapbooking, Nancy enjoys sewing dolls, traveling, gardening, and spending time with her family.

102

You must have been a Bee-u-tiful baby

designed by Nancy Freebairn

What a big wheel !
Chase - 2 yrs

STOP Beep Beep

designed by Nancy Freebairn

Treasury published by Sterling Publishing Co., Inc.

As a teacher, Dee has taught approximately 30,000 students personally and many more by means of four videos and four books about the craft. Additionally, she teaches rubber stamping to art and craft instructors of the United States Army in the U.S. and abroad.

Dee has her own line of stamps and owns and operates Posh Impressions, which is made up of two retail stores. She has served on two major industry-related advisory boards and is currently serving on the Hobby Industry Association (HIA) Board of Directors.

photo by Barber Photography

Dee Gruenig is an avid scrapbooker and is recognized as a master of innovation when it comes to adapting stamping accessories to create original stamping effects.

In 1989, Dee became the first to demonstrate rubber stamping to a television audience. She has since appeared numerous times on popular television craft shows. She has also been able to represent various product manufacturers and retailers.

Dee is the author of three very successful rubber stamping books, *Decorating Scrapbooks with Rubber Stamps*, *The Great Rubber Stamp Book*, and *Rubber Stamp*

designed by Dee Gruenig

103

...WAS SO FASCINATING OUTSIDE THE MILITARY CAMP. THE ART & BRUSH SHOPS WERE OUR FAVORITES!

designed by Dee Gruenig

Sea World

designed by Dee Gruenig

designed by Dee Gruenig

designed by Dee Gruenig

designed by Dee Gruenig

designed by Dee Gruenig

105

Rhonda Rainey is an artist of many interests and talents. She is an award-winning water colorist and designer. She is also the author of *Decorating with Paper & Paint* published by Sterling Publishing Co., Inc.

Those associated with Rhonda find her to be thoughtful and innovative when it comes to pushing the boundaries of established crafting techniques. She approaches each new project with a fresh and spirited perspective.

An art educator for twenty years, Rhonda is currently working as a free-lance artist and designer. She is the mother of three grown children and is a fun-loving grandmother. She resides in Idaho, where the rugged landscape and the quiet corners of nature provide subject matter for her work.

I do promise by the warmth of the sun, by the cool breezes of a spring morning, and by the wild flowers that are painted on the hillside. My love shall be as true as is the creation upon which we roam. . . . My love is as honest as the scent of the rose. I will love you as spring warms the earth, as the sunset embosses the mountain tops—each day and forever.

designed by Rhonda Rainey

designed by Rhonda Rainey

Our Family History

Hugh & Lorraine — married June 4, 1930
Charles & Geraldine — married Mar. 23, 1955
Charles Jr. & Laurie — married July 29, 1978
Michael & Julie — married June 27, 1980
Melanie & Kenneth — married Sept. 8, 1990
Leslie & Sebron — married Oct. 18, 1995
Patricia

Herman
Duffy
Boots

designed by Rhonda Rainey

Days Gone By

Out of the blue, Dad's cousin sent him a package full of photographs with a letter asking him if he might be able to identitfy some of the people and places pictured so she could record them in her family history.

What a wonderful time it was sitting with him and listening to the stories he told of days gone by. The childhood memories seemed to overflow as he described places he lived and people he knew and was fond of.

I just had to include them here in my scrapbook.

MEMORY IS YOUR LINK WITH THE CENTURIES. ALL THAT MEN HAVE REMEMBERED AND SET DOWN IN PRINT THROUGH THE AGES IS A PRECIOUS LEGACY TO YOU. THE MIRACLE OF MEMORY GIVES CONTINUITY TO LIFE.

designed by Rhonda Rainey

designed by Rhonda Rainey

Metric equivalency chart

mm-millimetres cm-centimetres
inches to millimetres and centimetres

inches	mm	cm	inches	cm	inches	cm
1/8	3	0.3	9	22.9	30	76.2
1/4	6	0.6	10	25.4	31	78.7
3/8	10	1.0	11	27.9	32	81.3
1/2	13	1.3	12	30.5	33	83.8
5/8	16	1.6	13	33.0	34	86.4
3/4	19	1.9	14	35.6	35	88.9
7/8	22	2.2	15	38.1	36	91.4
1	25	2.5	16	40.6	37	94.0
1 1/4	32	3.2	17	43.2	38	96.5
1 1/2	38	3.8	18	45.7	39	99.1
1 3/4	44	4.4	19	48.3	40	101.6
2	51	5.1	20	50.8	41	104.1
2 1/2	64	6.4	21	53.3	42	106.7
3	76	7.6	22	55.9	43	109.2
3 1/2	89	8.9	23	58.4	44	111.8
4	102	10.2	24	61.0	45	114.3
4 1/2	114	11.4	25	63.5	46	116.8
5	127	12.7	26	66.0	47	119.4
6	152	15.2	27	68.6	48	121.9
7	178	17.8	28	71.1	49	124.5
8	203	20.3	29	73.7	50	127.0

yards to metres

yards	metres	yards	metres	yards	metres	yards	metres	yards	metres
1/8	0.11	2 1/8	1.94	4 1/8	3.77	6 1/8	5.60	8 1/8	7.43
1/4	0.23	2 1/4	2.06	4 1/4	3.89	6 1/4	5.72	8 1/4	7.54
3/8	0.34	2 3/8	2.17	4 3/8	4.00	6 3/8	5.83	8 3/8	7.66
1/2	0.46	2 1/2	2.29	4 1/2	4.11	6 1/2	5.94	8 1/2	7.77
5/8	0.57	2 5/8	2.40	4 5/8	4.23	6 5/8	6.06	8 5/8	7.89
3/4	0.69	2 3/4	2.51	4 3/4	4.34	6 3/4	6.17	8 3/4	8.00
7/8	0.80	2 7/8	2.63	4 7/8	4.46	6 7/8	6.29	8 7/8	8.12
1	0.91	3	2.74	5	4.57	7	6.40	9	8.23
1 1/8	1.03	3 1/8	2.86	5 1/8	4.69	7 1/8	6.52	9 1/8	8.34
1 1/4	1.14	3 1/4	2.97	5 1/4	4.80	7 1/4	6.63	9 1/4	8.46
1 3/8	1.26	3 3/8	3.09	5 3/8	4.91	7 3/8	6.74	9 3/8	8.57
1 1/2	1.37	3 1/2	3.20	5 1/2	5.03	7 1/2	6.86	9 1/2	8.69
1 5/8	1.49	3 5/8	3.31	5 5/8	5.14	7 5/8	6.97	9 5/8	8.80
1 3/4	1.60	3 3/4	3.43	5 3/4	5.26	7 3/4	7.09	9 3/4	8.92
1 7/8	1.71	3 7/8	3.54	5 7/8	5.37	7 7/8	7.20	9 7/8	9.03
2	1.83	4	3.66	6	5.49	8	7.32	10	9.14

Index